*WHITE HOUSE NANNIE*

# WHITE HOUSE NANNIE

## MY YEARS WITH

## CAROLINE AND JOHN KENNEDY, JR.

## Maud Shaw

THE NEW AMERICAN LIBRARY

FIRST PRINTING

Published by The New American Library, Inc.
1301 Avenue of the Americas, New York, New York 10019
Published simultaneously in Canada by
General Publishing Company, Ltd.
A condensed version of this book first appeared in the
*Ladies Home Journal.*
Library of Congress Catalog Card Number: 66–17883
Printed in the United States of America

I WOULD LIKE *to acknowledge with appreciation the help and assistance received in compiling this book from Mr. Michael Borissow and Mr. Peter Whittle, of Southern News Services, Ltd., Maidstone, Kent, England.*

Maud Shaw

# *Illustrations*

# WHITE HOUSE NANNIE

# Chapter One

A GOLD-EMBOSSED, leather-bound scrapbook stands on the bookcase in my home in Sheerness, Kent, England. It is my proudest possession, not so much for the book with its costly binding—lovely though it is—but more for the inscription it contains, written by Mrs. Jacqueline Kennedy, widow of the late President Kennedy. It is a simple sentence, which I like to feel epitomizes nearly forty years of caring for other people's youngsters—words which now, in my retirement, can be treasured.

It says: "You brought such happiness to all our lives and especially to President Kennedy, because you made his children what they are."

The book was presented to me by Mrs. Kennedy on the day I left her and little John and Caroline, after seven and a half dramatic, moving and happy years. In that time I was privileged to know President John F. Kennedy, his wife and children in a way that only someone "living in" with the family could.

They were seven and a half momentous years in which pages of history were written by the young President. They were years of great achievement, grief, turmoil and tears.

I nursed the children from the cradle and came to love them just as if they had been my own. Happily they repaid me with their own love and affection.

For Mrs. Kennedy I always had great respect and admiration, which deepened into something more after the tragedy of her husband's death, as I saw the way she overcame her tremendous grief in the gaze of worldwide publicity to build a life anew.

President Kennedy was a man I felt honored to know. I say that with the deepest sincerity, for I always knew him to be a man of kindness and consideration. He was that rare combination of a successful yet simple man. As President of the United States, he shouldered the problems of the Western world, yet always he found time for his family and those near to him.

I always remember one particular time when the White House was in a pandemonium of activity, and the President was working late in his office, taking meals in his suite, completely surrounded by books and paperwork. He came along the corridor shortly after I had put the children to bed, when I was having a five minutes' sit-down on an ordinary hard-backed chair in the corridor.

"Hello, Miss Shaw," he said, smiling over the top of

an armful of papers. "Is that the best chair you can find to relax on?"

"Oh, I'm fine, Mr. President," I replied.

But he fussed around, and only when he was quite satisfied that I was perfectly comfortable did he return to pressing affairs of state. Only a small incident, yes, but one that was typical of the thoughtfulness of the man, despite his other cares.

Another occasion when he exhibited this kind of consideration for others amid the cares of his office, was when I was visited at the White House by the mother of an old friend. The old lady was over ninety and had lived in Germany most of her life, but she had dipped into her savings at this ripe old age to visit the United States for the first time. While having tea with me, she expressed her greatest wish—to shake hands with President Kennedy.

Feeling a little doubtful, I relayed the story to the President's secretary, Mrs. Lincoln, who in turn passed it on to the President. Sure enough, he came bounding out of his office, smiling all over his face like a little boy, to greet the old lady and happily pose for a picture with his arm around her shoulder. It must have been an irritating interruption, those ten minutes lost in the middle of his working day, but it meant so much to this total stranger, and he was "big" enough to realize it.

Looking back over my working life as I do in the following pages, it is not surprising that most of my memories are drawn from those years with the Kennedy family. But before joining the Kennedys, I lived and traveled in many parts of the world, meeting and living with many families, and helping to bring up their children. I have my particular memories of all these children; many of them still keep in touch quite regularly, and it is part of the fascination of my job to see them again when grown up and find out how they have changed and developed.

I hope to live long enough to see how John and Caroline grow up, although, having seen their personalities develop from the diaper stage to school age, I have a fair idea.

John, I am sure, will be active, outgoing and extrovert. Already, he has his father's self-confidence and charm with strangers. "I'm John F. Kennedy, Junior," he says when asked his name. Yet, like his father, his self-assurance is tempered with consideration for other people's feelings.

Caroline is the quieter, more reserved of the two, slow to make friends and preferring the company of people she knows to joining in with strangers. In this respect, she is like her mother, who, for all her worldly self-confidence, is at heart rather a shy person. Caroline, too, is sensitive to other people's feelings, quick to realize and make amends for having hurt anyone by something she has said or done.

Mrs. Kennedy cannot be right in saying that I made the President's children what they are, for they have inherited many characteristics from their parents. Yet, if in

4

those seven years I possibly imparted to them some of the things children should know and understand, then I am well satisfied.

Being a "foreigner," it has been a privilege to live with the Kennedy family through their greatest years, and while some of the memories have passed forever, some can never be forgotten. One day, in particular, is burned eternally on my mind. . . .

# Chapter Two

❀

❀  ❀

Nᴏᴠᴇᴍʙᴇʀ 22, 1963, ended the life of a very fine man, changed the lives of hundreds of others around him and, in varying degrees, affected almost everyone. But the news of the assassination of President John F. Kennedy cut through the lives of those of us in the White House in a way that was completely shattering. It took time for the reality to sink in, and then, when our minds thawed and we understood what had happened, most people there gave way to the emotion of that awful moment. I do not normally cry, but I wept for President Kennedy. So did his secretaries, Cabinet members, White House ushers, cooks, maids and Secret Service men. None of them would be ashamed to admit it. The death of this good, just, kind man affected us all; it was a feeling of intense personal loss.

After the first stunning shock came a period of frantic confusion inside the White House. Orders went out only to be countermanded immediately. Instructions were given and canceled. Rumors spread and were denied. Everyone seemed to race everywhere. Looking back, it seemed that we all wanted to do something, anything, at top speed, lest we had time to sit down and weep.

It was an incredible day. Even now, thinking back, I am overcome by the sadness of it all. So much happened that most of it is a blur, like a film run through a projector too fast. Yet many details will stay in my memory forever.

The day began perfectly normally, of course. As always, it started when Caroline came into my room first thing in the morning, followed shortly afterward by John. They both looked so sweet, a bit sleepy-eyed and tousled, their chatter punctuated by early-morning yawns.

"Good morning, Miss Shaw," they said, as usual. "May we get up now?" It was about seven o'clock then, so we all got up and went into the bathrooms to wash. Caroline dressed herself, and John only had to be helped with his buttons and shoes before the three of us went along to the dining room for breakfast. There was no hurry, for Caroline did not have to go to school in the solarium on the roof until nine, and she would not be going down to the ground floor to her father's office. Every day she had just ten minutes with him before joining her schoolmates on the White House lawn, but now, of course, the President and Mrs. Kennedy were away. So after a leisurely breakfast, Caroline went off to school, and John and I went for a walk during the morning.

The conversation at the lunch table revolved around their forthcoming birthdays. John would be three just three days later and Caroline six, two days after that. Lunchtime was a bit of an occasion that day, because we had guests—Senator Edward Kennedy's two children, Teddy and Kara, plus their nurse Miss O'Dowd—and we all ate together in the dining room.

Who could have guessed during the children's carefree chatter that this was to be the last normal meal any of us was to have in the White House?

Miss O'Dowd left with her two charges at about one-fifteen, and I was just thinking of putting John and Caroline to bed for their afternoon rest when the telephone rang in my room. It was an internal call, from Miss Nancy Tuckerman, Mrs. Kennedy's secretary.

"Miss Shaw?" Miss Tuckerman began, and then hesitated before going on. "I have some bad news for you. I'm afraid the President has been shot."

I had to ask her to repeat the message. It was not easy to grasp quite what she meant. The President shot? Impossible. But, yes, Miss Tuckerman was saying, the President had been shot while driving through Dallas, although no details were yet available. I remember saying something about hoping it was not serious, not thinking for one moment that he might be dead.

"That is all we know right now," Miss Tuckerman

*9*

said. "I'll call you back as soon as I hear how he is." I put down the phone, thinking what a terrible thing it was that anyone would try to shoot President Kennedy.

In this worried mood, I went back to John and Caroline, who were in the sitting room of the family suite. Caroline was reading a book, hunched up in an easy chair, and John was lying on his tummy, crayoning in a coloring book. It seemed the best thing to let them take their naps right away while I waited to find out just how badly their father had been hurt. There was no point in saying anything to them about it.

"Come along, children," I said, as brightly as possible. "It's time for your rest now." They were as good as gold and went to their rooms without protests. John, once tucked down in his bed, fell asleep, while Caroline lay on top of the covers, still reading her book. I went into my room for about twenty minutes, half expecting a call from Miss Tuckerman, but nothing happened. Oddly enough, it never crossed my mind to switch on the TV set. It was about two o'clock, and the inactivity was making me restless. I walked down the corridor toward the dining room and then saw one of the children's Secret Service detail, Bob Foster, leaning against the doorpost at the far end. He looked ghastly—pale-faced and ill.

He hardly moved as I walked up to him and asked: "What's the matter? Are you all right?" Never for a moment did I link the sight of him with the earlier phone call from Miss Tuckerman. When he looked up from the carpet his eyes were full of tears, and he stared blankly for what must have been several seconds before speaking.

"The President's dead."

That was all he said. Blunt, concise, straight to the heart. A hot-and-cold feeling swept over me as the shock of it hit, coupled with a peculiar, unreal sensation inside. Foster spoke again, and his voice seemed to come from miles away. "Sit down." He took my arm and sat me in one of the chairs in the corridor. Then he put a hand over his face, and I remember just sitting there as if for hours, trying to collect my thoughts, only vaguely aware of Bob Foster being present, big and suntanned as he was. The President was dead and there could be no mistake. The tragedy was written all over Foster's face. When at last the truth had sunk in, I got up and walked in a complete daze to my room.

Though not normally a person to cry easily, I wept for the death of this good, kindly, able man and for his wife, for whom this loss would be almost beyond bearing. And for the two little children in their rooms, one asleep, the other lost in a fairy tale, both blissfully unaware of the appalling tragedy which had struck into their tiny lives. Yes, the tears were most of all for them, these two little mites I had known almost from the moment they were born. Little Caroline, whom I had held in my arms at eleven days old and had nursed ever since. And John, whom I had talked of and planned for with Caroline even before he was born. I loved them both, and it broke my heart to think of the pain and shock that now lay in store for them.

To think that he would no longer call for them, his "John-John" and "Buttons," in those drawn-out Boston tones, and to realize that they would no longer see his face light up and grin at the sight of them—these recollections and others of a thousand similar moments oppressed me, and my black thoughts were not interrupted until about four o'clock, when Bob Foster reappeared. Poor Mr. Foster. I felt so sorry for him afterward, when I learned that the Secret Service men had drawn lots to see who should break the news to me, and he had lost. Apparently he had spent ten minutes screwing up his nerve to come and tell me, not knowing what he ought to say, which was why, in the end, he had just blurted out the news.

But there was no time for explanations when Foster knocked at my door and burst in almost immediately.

"Miss Shaw," he said. "We have to get out of the White House by six o'clock. Mrs. Kennedy is flying back from Dallas and doesn't want the children around when she gets back. Hurry now, we haven't much time."

He still looked very upset, but helped to get the three suitcases always kept ready in my room for such sudden moves. I began to throw some of my own things into my case—and then stopped to think.

"Where are we going?" I asked Foster, but before he could answer, the telephone rang.

*12*

Mrs. Ethel Kennedy, wife of then Attorney-General Robert Kennedy, was on the line. She asked first if we had heard the news. She sounded terribly upset and spoke very softly.

"I think you had better take the children to meet their mother," she said. "She is coming into Andrews Field at six."

I hesitated for a moment. It did not seem right to argue with anyone at that moment, but surely Mrs. Kennedy would not want to be met at the airfield by the children, who as yet knew nothing about their father's death.

"Oh, no," I said at last. "Surely not. I am sure Mrs. Kennedy would not want to see the children just now. Please don't ask that."

"All right—bring the children here," she said. "I can't think of anything else, can you? Anyway, I'll leave it to you. You know best what to do. . . ." She rang off.

Foster was still in the room and was obviously very agitated. His orders from somewhere above were to get the children out of the White House and, naturally, he was anxious to do so. It must have agonized him to see me standing there, numbed and not knowing which way to turn. He was kneeling on the floor by one of the suitcases, watching while I racked my brain to think of a place to take the children that would be away from the turmoil. Then it came to me. There was only one other person to turn to—the children's grandmother, Mrs. Janet Auchincloss, a naturally sympathetic woman with whom I had spoken in other moments of crisis.

I rang her number and she answered immediately. We spoke for a long time, our conversation interrupted from time to time because neither of us was able to stop crying. Mrs. Auchincloss was surprised that the children were to be moved from the White House, and although Mrs. Ethel Kennedy had invited us to her house, it might be better if the children went to stay with their "Grandmère" at this time, because it would be quieter there.

"Oh, yes, yes," Mrs. Auchincloss said. "Bring them over to me. This is the place for you all. Come and stay here. . . ."

She paused for a few moments, then spoke again, her voice more composed. "Miss Shaw, there is something I would like you to do, and I know my daughter would, too."

"Yes, of course. Anything."

"We feel you should be the one to break the news to the children, at least to Caroline."

"Oh, no," I said, "please don't ask me to do that." The idea filled me with horror.

"Please, Miss Shaw," Mrs. Auchincloss was saying. "It is for the best. They trust you, and you know how to deal with them. . . . I am asking you as a friend . . . please. It has to be you."

I stood silently for several moments, wondering about the prospect. It was the last thing in the world I wanted to do, and my immediate reaction was to continue to refuse. But then, quite suddenly, it came to me that I should be the one to tell Caroline. I did know that little girl so well, and perhaps it was my job to break the news. Finally I told Mrs. Auchincloss I would do so when we put her to bed that night.

It must have been after five by now, and we needed to hurry. With Mr. Foster's help, I began grabbing racks of the children's clothes and literally threw them into the suitcases. I took some of my own things—heaven knows what—and snapped the cases shut.

At this moment Caroline came in serenely, asking what all the fuss was about.

"We are going to Grand-mère's," I said, hoping it sounded like fun. "Go and get John. Hurry now, we are going to dinner and maybe we'll stay there to sleep."

Caroline grinned happily, hurried to fetch her brother and returned with him in a minute or so.

"Are we going to Grand-mère's?" he asked.

"Yes, and we must hurry. Mr. Foster is waiting." Bob Foster forced a smile, picked up the suitcases and took them along to the elevator. The children had a quick wash, changed into their street clothes and wrapped up well against the cold November wind.

We fairly tumbled into the elevator, arrived at the ground floor and hurried to the back door, where two big Secret Service limousines were waiting. The ground floor was a bedlam of people running and calling to each other, but I hurried the children along, talking to them all the time about nothing, anything—just anxious to get them into the car and away. We drove across Washington to Georgetown, and at the door of 3044 O Street, Mrs.

*15*

Auchincloss was waiting. She looked pale and had obviously been crying, but she received the children cheerfully and kissed them as affectionately as ever. It was almost dinnertime by now, and the children went into the dining room and sat down.

Mrs. Auchincloss had had no time to make preparations, so together we went upstairs to the guest bedroom, where the three of us were to stay. There was no crib for John, but Mrs. Auchincloss remembered an old one in the attic, and we brought it down and tried to assemble it in the guest room. It was so old and wobbly we had to tie it together with string. The maid assembled bedclothes for us all, we made the beds and then went down to dinner.

Still feeling heavy-hearted and close to tears, I could only pick at my food, but Caroline and John ate hungrily, chattering to each other. I was haunted by the thought that such carefree happiness would have to be shattered so soon.

It must have been seven-thirty—we had finished the meal and I was thinking of getting the children upstairs —when a Secret Service car drew up outside the house. A minute later, Mr. Foster was shown into the hall, and Mrs. Auchincloss went to meet him. He looked more harassed than ever. Even the cold November evening had brought no color to his face, and his eyes looked tired.

"Miss Shaw, I'm sorry, but we have to go back to the White House immediately," he said. "Mrs. Kennedy is

*16*

coming back tonight and wants the children in the house with her."

"But I thought . . ."

Mr. Foster interrupted me wearily. "I'm sorry. Everything else has been canceled. We have to go back."

Luckily, our cases had not been unpacked, and Mrs. Auchincloss reluctantly had them brought down while I got the children's coats. Caroline and John were still in the dining room, and I stepped outside to take a deep breath to compose myself.

"Children," I called, going into the room. "Dear me, what a night! We have to go back home now. Mummy wants us. Caroline, be my bestest friend and help John on with his coat." Caroline clapped her hand across her mouth to smother a giggle. It was all a big game.

"Come on, John-John," she said in her most motherly tone. "Put your coat on, we're going home again."

We said hurried good-byes to Mrs. Auchincloss and climbed back into the car. It drove quickly across the city and through the gates of the White House on Pennsylvania Avenue. Outside there were hundreds of people. Flashbulbs popped as we drove in.

"What are all those people there for?" Caroline asked.

"To see you," I said, and thankfully she did not ask any more questions.

We drew up at the back door and hurried in. The place was ablaze with lights, and the ushers who met us seemed

*17*

extra considerate now. One took my arm and helped me through the door. He said nothing, just shook his head and frowned, squeezed my arm and hurried away. Inside, all was still confusion, a blur of faces hurrying in all directions. I caught sight of Mr. West, the chief usher, sitting on a chair in the hall looking utterly lost. A secretary ran along the corridor still crying. There was a shout, and a babble of voices came from somewhere out of sight.

My head ached. I was trembling, and felt as if I could cry for days. It was like that, and, in fact, I did cry for days. It sounds unreal, maybe, but one couldn't help it. For many days, emotion was so heavy in the air at the White House that it needed only the sight of one person looking tearful to set two other people to weeping. Like many others, I eventually went to see the President's physician, Dr. Janet Travell. She gave me tranquilizers, which helped me to feel better and pull myself together.

The children hurried into the house and to the elevator while a Secret Service man followed with the baggage. On the second floor, there seemed to be more people than usual. No one seemed to know exactly when Mrs. Kennedy was returning to the White House. All anyone knew was that she was expected imminently.

As soon as we reached our rooms, the telephone rang and one of the ushers said that Mrs. Kennedy might first go to the Naval Hospital with the President's body. It was a good thing, in a way, for that diversion would give me time to get the children to bed—and to speak to Caroline.

But before they got into bed, the phone rang at least another half-dozen times, each time with different and contradictory messages from the ushers and Secret Service detail, doing their best to keep me informed of Mrs. Kennedy's movements. The confusion was incredible, and months later, when I talked with Mrs. Kennedy about that dreadful day, she told me that although she had definitely wanted the children near her when she got back from Dallas, she had above all wanted them undisturbed until they were told of their father's death.

Getting the children off to bed was a dreadful business. It was impossible to stay happy with them. Once I left them in the bath to go into my room just to be alone. I stared out of the window overlooking Pennsylvania Avenue. The crowd had thickened now, spilling over the road into Lafayette Square. The people stayed there all night.

Messages were still coming in on the phone, but by now I almost didn't care. I felt worn out, drained, tearful and so very, very sad. Outside in the corridors, feet were scuffing along quickly, and I moved slowly while the children were dried and dressed in their nightclothes. I was feeling more and more depressed every second, and hated the prospect of telling Caroline what she had to be told. By the time they were ready to run into their rooms, I could no longer smile or join in their talk.

Feeling overwhelmingly sad, I put John in his bed, said his prayers with him, tucked him down and went in to Caroline. I sat on the edge of the bed and felt tears

*19*

well up in my eyes. I started reading to her from one of her books—she loved this moment of the day—but after a few paragraphs I could no longer see the words. Caroline looked up at me, her little face frowning with concern.

"What's the matter, Miss Shaw? Why are you crying?"

I took her gently in my arms. "I can't help crying, Caroline, because I have some very sad news to tell you."

Then I told her what had happened. It was a dreadful time for us both.

Eventually she fell asleep while I sat on the bed, still patting her. At last I tiptoed from the room, leaving the door open just a crack, as always, and went into my own room next door.

By this time, according to the latest reports, Mrs. Kennedy should have been back at the White House. I rang the Secret Service detail and asked if she had returned. It appeared that she had gone to the Naval Hospital with the President's body and would be returning later that night. It was impossible to sleep, so I just sat up in my room all through the night, waiting and waiting. The hours ticked by slowly, and it was five-thirty and getting light when I finally decided that Mrs. Kennedy would not be returning and went to bed. As it happened, she came back only an hour afterward.

I did not sleep long. Caroline came into my room very early. She looked pale, and her big eyes were sad and puzzled. John still did not know and anyway was really too young to understand. (Later, it was decided that Mr. Robert Kennedy could best tell John what had happened.)

Somehow Caroline had the wisdom not to ask questions while John was about, but when he trotted off, the questions came thick and fast. I answered them quietly, trying not to go into the details which I had learned from the Secret Service men the night before. Both the children, of course, wanted to go in and see their mother early in the morning, but I told them she was resting and that it would be better if she was left to sleep.

Shortly before ten Mrs. Kennedy came to the nursery and took the children downstairs to the East Room, where they knelt and prayed before the President's casket. At ten, there was a private mass for the family, a few close friends and members of the White House staff. Caroline and John watched the mass through the open doors of the Green Room.

Somehow the day dragged through, and Mrs. Kennedy came back to the nursery at about four P.M. Her mother was with her, and they were both dressed in black. Silently, Mrs. Kennedy hugged her children, tears running freely down her pale cheeks. She said very little, and I really did not know what to say or do to try and comfort this unhappy woman.

"I'm so sorry. I wish there were something I could do for you," was all I could manage.

Mrs. Kennedy tried to smile. "Just keep the children happy," she replied. "That is all you can do for me. As

*21*

long as I know they are happy, it will be a great help."

It has always struck me, since then, how terribly logical children can be. Some of the questions Caroline asked could only have come from a child, and they had to be answered plainly and without emotion, for to her they were real problems. When she went down to the Capitol to see her father's casket lying in state, she asked a number of questions, and only by replying to every question logically did I think the child could be eased in her mind. It seemed essential never to try to sidestep any of her questions.

John was too young, of course, to understand everything that was happening. The day before the President's funeral, when Mrs. Kennedy went to the Capitol to kneel by his casket, she took Caroline in with her, while I went with John and Mr. Foster for a walk around the building. One of the Capitol officials showed us around and led us into a big office to wait until Mrs. Kennedy was ready to leave. In the office, John's attention was immediately attracted to a large board decorated with miniature flags of all nations, and our guide asked John if he would like one.

"Yes, please," he said. "And one for my sister, please." He was always so good like that, remembering his sister. The official let him pick out two flags, and then John hesitated.

"Please, may I have one for Daddy?"

We exchanged glances and I nodded to the official. John picked one. It was rather strange, I thought, that his choice should be a flag almost identical to his father's personal standard, although that flag itself was not among the collection. However, he must have remembered what the President's standard was like, for the one he chose was very similar.

Later that night, I told Mrs. Kennedy about this incident and said: "Would you like the flag?"

"Yes, please," she said. "I'd like that."

That little memento was later buried with the President. It seemed to me so poignant and fitting, for President Kennedy was buried on his son's third birthday.

# Chapter Three

❀

❀   ❀

ONLY A WEEK after President Kennedy had been buried, we began moving out of the White House. It seemed as if Mrs. Kennedy could not get out of the place quickly enough once she had recovered from the initial shock of her husband's death. For that week she saw visitors, attended to her affairs and came to play with the children, but it was clear that she was doing these things almost automatically. She had been offered houses by friends in New York and Washington, and, since she did not want to go back to her home in Hyannis Port, she finally decided to accept the offer of Mr. and Mrs. Averell Harriman to borrow their home on N Street in Georgetown, Washington.

All around us, changes were taking place in the White House. Vice-President Lyndon Johnson, sworn in as President Kennedy's successor, was moving in. Within a day of the assassination, the late President's personal papers were removed from his office by his secretary, Mrs. Lincoln.

New faces appeared in the White House corridors. Old faces disappeared forever. The changeover from the old administration to the new seemed to be swift and almost merciless, but I suppose there cannot be too much sentiment at the top.

Up on the second floor, I felt a little lost, but I did everything possible to keep the children happy. It was the only thing I could do to help Mrs. Kennedy. Since the children had missed their previously planned birthday parties, we held a combined party for them about a week later, and Mrs. Kennedy came down to that noisy little affair, dressed simply in a black cocktail dress, without jewelry.

She still looked pale and drawn, but smiled for the first time since the tragedy hit her. John and Caroline each had about eight little friends, and we sat them at separate tables, with a birthday cake for each group. We sang "Happy Birthday" to them both and waited on the tables, joining in their games after they had all eaten. Mrs. Kennedy chuckled aloud when John took a huge breath to blow out his three candles, but the sadness was still heavy in her eyes as she watched over her children.

"I'm glad they are happy," she said quietly when I stood next to her, watching the children singing and opening their presents. "Thank you for all you have done."

I took the opportunity to ask her when we would be

moving from the White House. She took a long look round the room, with its wallpaper depicting the War of Independence, scenes which had always fascinated John, and suddenly seemed to make up her mind. "I want to go as quickly as possible," she said.

The incoming First Lady, Mrs. Lady Bird Johnson, had told Mrs. Kennedy to take her time in moving out, but from the moment she made up her mind to go, Mrs. Kennedy worked frantically to pack up her home and get away.

Every porter, maid and hired hand in the White House was set to packing furniture and stripping the rooms of Mrs. Kennedy's personal effects—her china, porcelain, pictures, linen, chairs (including the President's rocking chair), carpets and the million and one things she had moved into the Presidential home during her three-year occupation. It was heartbreaking to see each room slowly stripped and skimmed of all the beautiful things she had so patiently arranged throughout the house. Trucks began drawing up at the doors of the White House, and men filed in and out with packing cases. I saw the President's rocking chair for a moment, sitting on the lawn before it was lifted into a van—just one of the sadder touches which brought home the real fact that we were preparing to leave the White House for good.

Up in the nursery, I had started sorting out the children's clothes and toys. It was a difficult task, for we would need some of them right away in the Harriman house and other stuff a couple of weeks later when we went down to Palm Beach for Christmas. The children's closets appeared to be packed with thousands of items not seen for months.

At one stage, I was literally knee-deep in toys in John's room, and my head spun with the problem of trying to get it all packed and removed. The ever-willing Secret Service men ran to find packing cases, cardboard boxes, trunks and anything else they could lay their hands on that would hold toys, clothes, books and all the other paraphernalia of the nursery.

At one stage, Mr. West, the chief usher, had to be asked for more help.

"I'm sorry, Miss Shaw," he said. "But I'm afraid everyone is working to get Mrs. Kennedy's effects packed."

"But we're moving too!" I said. "There's nearly as much stuff to pack for the children as for Mrs. Kennedy." In the end, two more maids were enlisted to help, but even so my back was absolutely breaking by the time it was finished. There were then almost forty packing cases and boxes of toys and children's things. And I had to know where everything was.

The children helped as best they could, but being children, they were reluctant to pack anything of their own. Things had to be put into boxes when they weren't looking. Little John wailed when he saw some of his favorite toys being packed, and it was necessary to get quite secretive about it with him, lest he unpack the boxes behind my back!

As it was, three boxes had to be undone when Caroline's favorite doll, Raggedy-Ann, was missing. I could not remember having touched it, but this little dolly was Caroline's constant companion and had to be found. After I had undone the three boxes and spread the contents all over the nursery floor, we found the doll under Caroline's bed! It was incredible how we kept on coming across little treasures the children had mislaid months before, and the "reserved" pile of toys they wanted to carry with them grew to a mountainous stack before my foot went down and they all went into yet another box.

Everyone was genuinely sad when the Kennedys left the White House, and the sorrow expressed by all the staff at our having to go in such tragic circumstances was quite overwhelming. The Kennedys had always treated everyone very well; it had always been their aim, it seemed, to be as little trouble to the staff as possible.

On many occasions, Mrs. Kennedy would eat her dinner with the children, without bothering the cooks or the butlers to make a separate meal for her. "No, don't bother to cook me anything," she used to say. "I'll eat with the children. If it is good enough for them, I know it will be fine for me."

The President, too, had been no bother to anyone. When, perhaps, Mrs. Kennedy was away on an official trip, he would sit in his favorite armchair with a meal on a chairside tray, eating his dinner with his children playing on the floor around him.

Both of them had that simple approach. They could

have asked for, and got, anything in the world they fancied, but they nearly always preferred to live simply in their off-duty moments. This is why Mrs. Kennedy rearranged the second floor of the White House to accommodate her family closely together, in a separate compartment as it were. Away from public duties, John Kennedy and his wife were uncomplicated people, perfectly happy and quite absorbed in their own company and that of their lovely children.

And there is no doubt that the staff came to adore Caroline and John. The two children were always well-behaved, polite and considerate. Being the children of the President, they could easily have made life miserable for the staff, but they never did. When we left, the kitchen staff begged us to take the children back to visit them. John had been a particular favorite, forever trotting into the kitchens to play with the pots and pans, rifling the shelves to get down egg poachers, milk pans and things like that to make a little shop or a kitchen of his own in the corner. He used to play for hours in there, and the chefs and kitchen maids would play with him, making the little chap chuckle at their antics in his "shop."

I, too, was miserable at leaving this vast house, which had become my home three years before. I would be losing all my friends there, and the little jokes and intimacies we had shared. Never again would I be kidded along by the policemen at the gates, who used to pull my leg whenever I returned after a day off.

"Hey, you can't come in here," they would say. "You're English, you don't live here."

"All right," I'd retort. "If you don't let me in, you'll have to look after the children. See how long you last at that."

Those days, those memories, will live with me forever, for they were some of my happiest. Only once after leaving the White House did I return—weeks later, to collect some personal documents, I think—and the only sensation was an oppressive feeling of melancholy at walking through those familiar portals and feeling a complete stranger.

The day we finally left was gray and overcast, the elements staging a perfect backdrop for the occasion. It was cold, and snow was in the air; the last of the leaves had been blown off the trees around the lawns. Our rooms looked equally bleak and bare; all our personal things had been carried off, except for a couple of suitcases for myself and the children. Mrs. Kennedy came out of her suite and along the corridor to meet us as we walked toward the elevator.

"All set?" she asked.

"Yes," I replied. There was a lump in my throat as I walked down the corridor, knowing that we would never retrace these footsteps. At the elevator, I looked back toward the nursery rooms, where I had shared three such happy years with the children. The rooms were quite silent now. A pall of sadness hung like a dust sheet over everything.

"Come along." Mrs. Kennedy touched my arm and motioned me into the lift. We rode down in silence, lost in memories. Even the children said nothing until we got into the car and drove down the pathway, followed by our Secret Service car. At the South Gate, the children, as always, prepared to wave to the patrolman on duty. Their favorite was a huge, kind cop called Pete.

"Where's Pete?" Caroline asked as we swept up to the gate.

"I expect he's off duty today," I said.

"Oh, I wish I could wave good-bye to him," the little girl said. But we were through the open gates before she could say any more.

Sixteen Hundred Pennsylvania Avenue, Washington, D.C., was a closed world to us now, and I felt like crying.

# Chapter Four

I HAVE BEEN working now for almost forty years with all sorts of people and their children in many parts of the world. But in the first place, I really had to fight hard to go out to work at all.

Growing up in Malta with my parents and my younger brothers and sisters—John, Minnie, Harry and Hettie—I had always led a rather sheltered kind of existence. My father was in charge of the boilermaking plant at the naval dockyard, and he, being a strong-minded sort of person, always said that his daughters would never need to go out to work.

He had been a seafaring man during the early part of his life, and settled down in Malta with his family when I was only four. He had done so, he always said, so that he could have his family about him, and he saw no reason why either of us girls should go out to work. And to be perfectly honest there really wasn't any need for me to do so—except that I was bored; I also wanted to be able to buy the kind of dresses I particularly liked and not have to depend on Father. But Father wouldn't hear of the idea at first. My mother was an equally forceful person, though, and it was she who persuaded him to allow me to find a job.

But what to do? There were a few shops in Valletta where I might have worked, but very little else. The situation seemed rather hopeless until friends mentioned that a family living not too far away from us, across the harbor, needed a governess for their small child, aged five.

It seemed a good idea. I knew enough about children, having helped to bring up my brothers and sisters, so I caught the ferry across the harbor and called on the family to offer my services.

Major McCausland of His Majesty's Royal Marines and his wife were immediately very friendly, and their little girl was delightful. They asked me to take the job (at twelve shillings a week!) and within a few days, I had certainly done what I set out to do—achieve my independence. But I felt terrible about it. The trouble was that with having to stay in to look after the child all day, and most evenings when the McCauslands went out, I badly missed the social whirl I had been used to. I felt like a caged lion.

However, I got used to it. I could always console myself with the thought that if things did get too bad, it would only cost me a penny on the ferry to get back home. Throughout my life, as far as possible, I have always tried to keep to one piece of fatherly advice which stuck in my mind: "Always have your fare home, girl" —though it was never again just a penny.

It was during an afternoon gossip in the park with other governesses—we called it our "grapevine"—that I heard of a certain Captain Miller, an Army man and his wife, who were looking for a governess for their two year old. They were going back to England for a short while and then on to Germany. Influenced perhaps by my father's seafaring tales, I have always had an irresistible urge to travel, which is probably the reason why I have rarely stayed in any job more than a couple of years. (The seven years with the Kennedys was by far the longest time I ever stayed with any one family, but they were very special years, close to my heart.) So I took the job, and by a roundabout route, via Port Said, headed north to England.

Having lived practically all my life in Malta, the shock of an English winter was terrible. It was November when we landed at Southampton, and the biting cold was quite a new experience. Thankfully we were only in England in that sort of weather for about a week. We then left for Baüschalber, where Captain Miller was attached to the British Rhineland Occupation Force.

We took up residence on the side of a beautiful wooded mountain, quite one of the most delightful spots I have ever known. Whenever possible, I used to go up to the top of the mountain and sit and watch the deer run-

*35*

ning through the trees. A farmer worked there, way up in the hills, and he used to sing with an extraordinarily beautiful voice. It was all so peaceful, restful and relaxing.

Life felt wonderful then. I was 23, independent, living in a beautiful country and very happy with my work. This was the beginning of my secret ambition, not yet fully appreciated, to see the world, and I managed to take in a lot of the country during my time there.

For a year with the Millers in Germany, I had hardly a care in the world. But then they announced they were moving to India. For some reason I never understood, my father had always told me never to visit India. It was one of those strongly implanted childhood things, and, even though I never really knew the reason, I shied away from the idea of going to that country. Rather desolately (for I wanted to stay with the Miller family), I decided to return to England. There I found myself—two thousand miles from home, terribly lonely, with no job, little money and no idea of where or how I was going to live. It was not my happiest moment!

But even in those days, good nannies were hard to get, and I soon found myself with a choice of positions. I stayed in England until the war and, over the years, worked with many families and had many pleasant experiences—and some funny ones.

Once, when I was unhappy with a family—the woman made life a misery for all the domestic servants—the agency telephoned to say that a family living only about fifty yards from my present address would like to see me. The agency proprietress called them for me and made an appointment for the following afternoon. I decided I'd get there somehow, though getting out of the house might be a difficult task, for I was never allowed a free moment.

The following day I set off earlier than usual to pick up the little boy from school, having put on my best dress and rehearsed what I was going to tell Mrs. Spurway, my prospective employer. It was rather worrying because I had no references, my only copies having been torn up by my employer, who had also refused to give me one of her own.

It turned out that I did not need a reference, for the Spurways' Alsatian dog got me the job!

I met this animal, or rather, it met me the moment I began to walk up the Spurways' drive—a very fierce, tan-colored Alsatian. It came bounding out of a hedge, barking and growling. I was absolutely terrified, and it took all the courage I possessed not to run back down the drive. There seemed to be nowhere to hide, and so I simply stood still and let the dog come up and sniff my ankles, while murmuring things like "good dog" to him and patting him on the head.

After that he was quite friendly, and trotted up the drive behind me. I was surprised to be met on the doorstep by the lady of the house and her little daughter.

They both noticed my obvious pallor, and before either I or Mrs. Spurway could say anything at all, the little girl piped up: "I like you."

Mrs. Spurway laughed and explained: "We watched you coming up the drive from the window. I liked the way you handled Peter [the dog], and I think you are going to be the sort of intelligent and resourceful young lady we need." It was certainly the strangest introduction I ever had to a job!

After a chat, we shook hands on the appointment, and I then explained the predicament of never being able to get out of the house where I now worked. "I just can't see how I'm going to get away myself, let alone with all my luggage and chattels," I said.

I told her it would require at least two or three journeys for me to complete the move, and chances were that once I'd left the house for the first time, I'd never get back in again.

"Never mind," said Mrs. Spurway. "I have an idea. I'll send Arnold the gardener over for you."

It was rather a mystery how this was going to work, but any help was welcome. I gave in my notice and waited for the following Friday evening when I was due to move. Sure enough, just after tea, the Spurways' gardener appeared in the drive with his wheelbarrow.

Well, as transport it was a bit crude, but I loaded my cases on, hopped onto the top of them and, much to the horror of my late employer, rode to the Spurways like the Queen of the May! And after a triumphal entrance, I got on famously with the family, particularly the dog Peter. As it turned out, I was the only person he never barked at. We went everywhere together, and I must confess that in the end, I loved the dog just a little more than the child.

It was while I was living with a family in an apartment on Cromwell Road that I struck up a firm friendship with a London roadsweeper. Shades of Mary Poppins! It was not the thing a children's nurse would normally do.

This lovable little Cockney was a great talker, and we had some wonderful long chats together when on afternoon outings with young Richard, the little boy I was looking after at that time. In fact, our acquaintance began through Richard, when I accidentally tipped him out of his Victoria—a sort of pram-*cum*-pushchair. I was trying to get the thing up the curb, and poor little Richard went flying onto the pavement. Although he didn't hurt himself much, he was very, very indignant.

"You tipped me out of my Victoria!" he yelled accusingly. Well, while I felt sorry for the little chap, I simply couldn't help laughing at his outrageous expression. Then my roadsweeper appeared and helped to get Richard back into the conveyance, by which time all three of us were practically helpless with laughter. Most afternoons after that, the three of us would walk side by side together on the way to the park, me with the pushchair and the roadsweeper with his barrow. He never appeared to do much sweeping, but he was jolly good company!

I have never had any regrets about the numerous positions I have held in my time, for there has always been something to be learned in every household, and there has been enormous benefit from this richly varied experience.

I like children. It's as simple as that, and I suppose it is just as well, since it is the very foundation of this job of mine. It is a very rewarding job, for everything you put into it you get back from the children themselves. But it is exacting too, for you do have to put a lot into it if you are going to do it properly.

You give up a lot of time for them, even after they are packed away for the night and sleeping in their beds. There are always things to do for them and if you love them, as I came to love the little ones I looked after, you have to be prepared to sacrifice a lot of your own life for them. Every mother knows this, of course, and really, that is what my job is about. I am a mother-by-proxy to the little ones.

If I had to list the basic qualities for being a children's governess or nurse, they would be in this order:

1. A love of children.
2. A sense of fair play.
3. The ability to discipline them without tears.
4. The understanding that each child is different and should be handled and treated differently.

It is hard but wonderful work, heartwarming and intensely satisfying. When you love a child, he knows it, and gives back to you all the love and trust and affection that you give him. You can't ask much more from life than to be that important to an innocent little creature like a child, can you?

The only difficulty I have come across is when, as occasionally happens, a mother starts resenting the fact that her child is overfond of you. There was one time when a charge of mine, little Joey, fell down and cut his knee and came crying straight to me rather than to his mother for comfort. This upset his mother a lot, and, never wanting to usurp a mother's affections in any child's heart, I felt awful about it.

I think this two-way pull of affection, and the friction that it can generate between a mother and a child's nurse, is the thing that always worried me most. It is simply jealousy on the part of a mother, and, while very understandable, it is really a pity. After all, since a nannie is paid to take on most of a mother's duties in a child's life, it is only natural at times that a child should turn to its nannie for comfort rather than to its mother.

I prefer the little ones myself, say up to the age of eight years, because they are so much more interesting then. Older children, especially Americans, are by no means easy to control, because it seems to me they are given far too much freedom when they are very young. However, no two children are ever exactly the same; each has a personality of his own. It has always seemed important to adapt oneself to the particular personality of the child in one's care. John and Caroline Kennedy, for instance, have vastly different personalities. I suppose the three-year age difference is part of the answer here, but it seemed strange to find the contrasts in them so marked.

I remember a good example of what one can do with a child if one has the right approach. An Army captain and his wife, stationed in Gibraltar, had asked me to look after their son. His name was Michael—"Mikie," they called him—and when I arrived on "The Rock," Mikie was regarded as a bit of a terror. He did not seem to have any friends and did not get invitations to go to tea with the children of other Army families. Other nurses told me: "He's such a terrible influence on the other children. He won't eat, he's a nuisance and no one seems to be able to control him."

Mikie had had two nurses before me, and it appeared that the first one had let him do almost anything he liked, while the next had frightened the life out of him with her too strict discipline. Amazingly, we seemed to hit it off from the start. He met me at the docks with his parents and immediately shook hands and said: "Come along, I'll show you my house."

That night, I put him to bed and told him that in the morning he should be quiet and not get up until the Spanish maid brought in my tea, but that then he could put on his dressing gown and play with his toys. In the morning that is exactly what he did, and his parents were amazed! They were even more surprised when Mikie sat down and ate a good breakfast.

"But he never eats breakfast," his mother told me. "We always gave him a tin of biscuits first thing in the morning to keep him quiet." His father, a captain in an infantry regiment, was equally amazed. "What have you done to him?" he asked.

All one could say was that Mikie was being treated the same as any child should be—with kindness, fairness and without screaming or shouting at him. It is the real secret of caring for children. Treat them in a quiet manner, never bully, always be fair, tell them in a reasonable way what you expect of them and they will respond. Do the opposite and they will "play you up" unmercifully. Above all, children like to feel secure with the people who take care of them, so that they can put all their faith and trust in you.

I think I was more reluctant to part with Mikie than with any other child I have ever cared for, excepting perhaps John and Caroline Kennedy. In his case, it was a war that intervened.

I was still in Gibraltar at the end of July, 1939, when it was becoming pretty obvious to everyone in Europe that war with Germany could not much longer be avoided. Being a strategic military garrison, Gibraltar was alive with rumors, but none of them became fact until early August, when the Captain's regiment was ordered back to England and we were evacuated from "The Rock."

# Chapter Five

I JOINED MY FAMILY, who were by this time back in Sheerness, Kent, Mother having returned there after the death of my father ten years before. My sister Hettie and brothers Jack and Harry had come back too, and the men both went to work in the Sheerness naval dockyard. There was not a great call for children's nurses at the time, and in any case, people were being directed to war work. I applied to join the Wrens—Women's Royal Naval Service—but they took ages to call me up for service. I was still waiting when an advertisement appeared in *The Times*, asking for an English governess to go to Cyprus to look after the child of a Greek couple. This seemed better than sitting about waiting for something to happen, so I applied for the job, and inside a couple of weeks found myself on the way to Cyprus, overland through Europe.

It makes me shudder now to think of that trip, for

there I was, blissfully meandering through France in the early days of May, 1940—a matter of days before Hitler's Blitzkrieg offensive smashed through that country. If I had realized what was about to happen, I should never have gone. I most certainly would not have hung about Paris for a day, looking at the shops and drinking coffee on the boulevards!

Unfortunately, things did not continue to go too well for me that summer. It was beautiful on the island of Cyprus, of course, and there was a lot of fun to be had with the children and the other nurses, such as riding donkeys in the pinewood mountains. But in the home, conditions became very difficult with the Greek woman for whom I was working. We had totally different ideas on how to do things; there were arguments, and it all became unbearable.

By then there was no question of leaving for England, for Europe had been overrun by the Germans, and it was just not possible to buy a steamer ticket on the next boat to England—there weren't any tickets or any boats. But if it was not possible to leave the island, at least I could change my job, and did so. Once more, the governesses' grapevine started to work, and I soon found a new home with an utterly charming British family in Kyrenia. The woman, Mrs. Beryl Stracey, was widowed shortly after I joined the family, and, probably because of this, we became very close—more like friends than employer and employee.

She had two children, a girl of eleven named Ramona

and a boy, Simon, aged three. We lived quite happily in the Mediterranean sunshine until early in 1941, when the war caught up with us again. The authorities decided that Cyprus, being a British military base, had to be cleared of civilians. So once more, I packed up a home and embarked, this time on a troopship. From then on, the war kept me and the Straceys moving. Port Said, Cairo, Cape Town and back to Port Said again. When it got too dangerous for the children to remain in Cairo, Mrs. Stracey, feeling she ought to continue her work for the Navy, asked me if I would go to South Africa and take her children with me until the end of the war.

"It is entirely up to you," she said. "But I think I am of more use here, and anyway, the children love you and I know they would be happy with you. Will you take them?"

It was an extraordinary request, but remember, it was wartime. It took me no more than a few minutes to make up my mind that Ramona and Simon were as much my responsibility as anyone's in the circumstances.

We sailed from Aden just before Christmas, 1941, a couple of weeks after Pearl Harbor.

It was a big responsibility, although Ramona and Simon showed absolute trust in me, and I had no qualms about taking care of them in their mother's absence. We settled into a hotel in the Rondabosch district of Cape Town, quite near General Smuts's summer home, the gardens of which were open to the public and where we spent many happy afternoons in the warm South African

*47*

sunshine. Ramona went to a boarding school run by a sect of nuns, and came home most weekends. With Simon still under school age, we became a very happy family unit and stayed in South Africa for the rest of 1942.

It was mid-1943 before we managed to book passage to dear old Port Said (I knew that place better than I knew London), and it was not until May, 1944, that we were notified there would be room for our little group on the troopship *Devonshire*, which was sailing for England. We landed in Liverpool on June 6, 1944, the very day the Allied soldiers were landing in Normandy—D-Day.

The prospect of returning home and seeing my family and country after so many years away was an enticing one, but it was a sad homecoming for me. The sight of England after five years of war affected me terribly. Liverpool, being one of the principal ports for the Atlantic convoys, had been badly blitzed, and the gaping holes between houses told their own story of suffering.

Our landing in Liverpool meant saying good-bye to the Stracey children, for their home was on the south coast of England, while mine was on the southeast coast, and such were the stringent regulations enforced during the time of the D-Day invasion that no one was allowed to enter coastal zones unless it was absolutely imperative.

Never having lived under the harsh conditions of wartime Britain, I found it difficult to adjust to ration books and the meager amounts of goods they represented. After two eggs a day for breakfast, for instance, the shock of finding I was entitled to only one a week was considerable. Two ounces of butter did not go very far—neither did about six ounces of meat. Then, there were clothes. They were rationed by clothing coupons, which allowed one to buy no more than a couple of dresses and a coat every year, and stockings (when you could find them).

For the first time in my life, I found I was not allowed to go and get myself a job, as "nannie" was considered a nonessential occupation. I had to go down to Sheerness Labor Exchange and sign on to be directed to some work essential to the war effort. At first, I was told I would have to go into an electrical factory and help make aircraft components, but before being actually drafted, my sister Hettie, who was working in a children's nursery (the government had set up these nurseries to allow mothers to work in the factories), suggested that I take a job with her. It seemed more my line than working in a factory, so I applied and was accepted.

In 1946, when the war nurseries were closed down, I hankered to travel again. One or two inquiries had been started with agencies in London when, right out of the blue, a letter came from a friend in South Africa. She wrote to say that she knew of a post with the family of an oilman in England who was shortly going to Iran— would I like to go? Coming as it did on a cold winter's day, the letter was a godsend, for it offered me the chance to get back into the sunshine again. And what sunshine! At times it was 120 degrees in the shade in Abadan, Iran, where I ended up for the next three years.

In 1948 my mother fell ill. My sister Hettie was in America at the time, and I returned home to stay for two years. Unfortunately, my mother died in 1949 after a long illness, a remarkable woman who had always been very calm but at the same time strong-willed. Even though I had spent most of my life away from home, I felt that a "sheet anchor" had gone, and missed her very much.

Hettie, having spent a couple of years in America, returned home soon after and convinced me that I would enjoy life there. She told me that good positions were available quite readily, since the Americans liked English governesses for their children. I made some inquiries at a London agency specializing in domestic situations in the United States, and confirmed that it would not, indeed, be difficult to get a good job. That decided me. I would turn my wandering feet westward.

Getting into the United States was an incredibly difficult business, with endless journeys to the U.S. Embassy in Grosvenor Square, to fill in yards and yards of forms, undergo X-ray examinations, medical checkups and verbal cross-examinations from Immigration officials, and to provide references, photographs, passport, birth certificate and heaven knows what else.

Finding a job in America proved by far the easiest part of it. A few days after contacting the agency in London, I had an appointment to see Mr. Arthur Watson of Connecticut, one of the family that owns the big International Business Machines corporation. The thought of

1. Two-and-a-half-year-old Caroline, bored with her father's press conference, plays with a neighbor's dog. For her, politics did not interfere with the pleasant summer of 1960 at Hyannis Port.

2. What a day this was for all of us! November 9th, 1960, and Senator Kennedy has just become President-elect Kennedy. Here he walks with Caroline on the lawn of their Hyannis Port house.

*United Press International Photo*

*Wide World*

3. Coming out of church in Georgetown, President-elect Kennedy takes care of Caroline's doll as she independently walks on ahead.

4. Caroline and her father go for a stroll in Georgetown. This morning Caroline's "birthday present" came—her baby brother John!

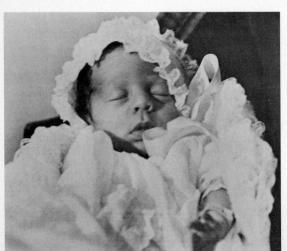

5. John Fitzgerald Kennedy, Jr., sleeps peacefully after his baptism. His father wore the same dress when he was baptized in 1917, and the bonnet belonged to his mother, Jacqueline, when she was an infant.

*Wide World Photos*

6. Off we go to Palm Beach for the warm and happy Christmas of 1960.

7. A loving greeting for Caroline, from her grandfather. Mr. Joseph P. Kennedy, always generous and hospitable, made our stays in Palm Beach delightful.

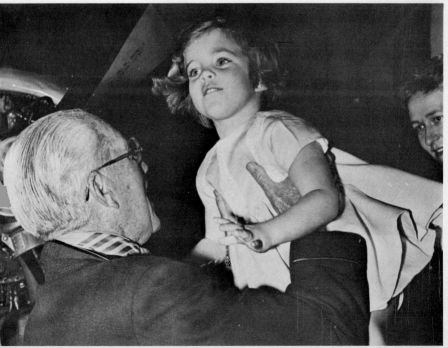

9. *(left)* Some people thought that when Caroline walked into her father's press conference wearing her mother's shoes, it was a publicity act. Far from it! It was no more than a little girl taking pleasure in dressing up.

8. *(above)* Caroline hardly seems to mind a snowless Christmas.

10. A lovely picture of Mrs. Kennedy and her daughter —and assorted friends.

. Count them. Ten! Though only
ree at this time, Caroline proved
adept and helpful assistant to me and
as never happier than when she was
lowed to sit and nurse her John-John.

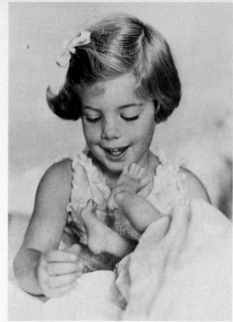

. *(below)* First friend at the White
ouse. Mrs. Kennedy thoughtfully
ked the White House gardener to
ild this charming snowman to greet
e children on their arrival at
00 Pennsylvania Avenue.

13. Mrs. Kennedy and John in the first official picture of John, taken on his first birthday.

14. A happy little soul.

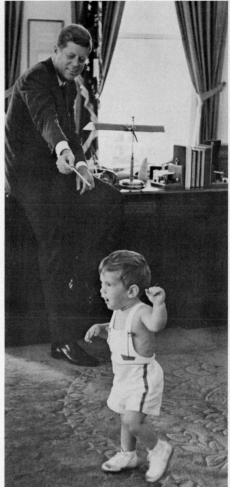

15. *(left)* Four-year-old Caroline wears a tarantella-dancer's costume in Ravello, Italy. She and her mother spent a sunny vacation visiting Mrs. Kennedy's sister, Lee Radziwill, at this seaside resort.

16. *(right)* After breakfast I always took the children down to see the President in his office. He never failed to have time to romp with them for a bit before Caroline went off to school.

Wide World Photos

Cecil W. Stou

17. *(left)* Two great horsewomen. Mrs. Kennedy shows Caroline, astride her favorite pony, Macaroni, the silver pin and blue ribbon she won for her performance in the walk-trot-jump class at a pony rally. 18. *(right)* Emergency repairs to Caroline's h on the beach at Hyannis Port. For two months in the summer, the children practically lived in the water along with all the other children of the Kennedy clan.

19. The Kennedy warmth and spirit certainly comes through here.

meeting my first genuine American millionaire was highly intriguing—I had conjured up a mental picture of a big man in a Stetson, chewing an enormous cigar and wearing an eye-blinding tie. But Mr. Watson could not have been more different—or more charming. He was conservatively dressed, soft-spoken and most kind. He showed me photographs of his wife and little daughter Ann, then sixteen months old, described his home in New Canaan, Connecticut, and said he would be delighted if I would take the job of caring for his little girl. We agreed, and I was soon on my way to America.

Mr. Watson met me at the dock and drove me in his huge motor car through New York to Connecticut. The drive up to New England was beautiful. I did not know quite what to expect of America, but the first impressions were of green pastures, trees, space and fresh air. Indeed, we might have been driving through rural Kent, three thousand miles away in Old England.

But the really impressive thing about America was the Americans themselves. Having traveled halfway round the world working with different people in all sorts of conditions, I found it was always the first few hours that colored one's attitude to a country and its people. In America, the Watsons made me like them and their homeland from the very outset, and I enjoyed my stay with them immensely.

The friends I had in the States all worked in New York or Washington, and one close friend, Constance Boden, kept urging me to go down to Washington with her, where, she said, a good position could easily be found. As beautiful and comfortable as it was in Connecticut, I eventually made up my mind to take the plunge and seek my fortune in Washington, D.C.

I grew to love that city, and to appreciate the delightful way in which it had been planned. All the architecture seems to fit together somehow. There are great blocks and blocks of government offices, naturally, but they have been designed and built with care so that they are easy on the eye, in contrast to the architectural jumble of, say, Whitehall. Even the post offices in Washington are pleasant to look at. Furthermore, the city has great natural beauty—lovely parks and open spaces, like the tidal basin on the Potomac River where the famous cherry blossoms turn the whole area pink in spring.

Another pleasant place to visit—and where later I very often took Caroline and John Kennedy—was Dumbarton Oaks, a huge estate open to the public, with beautiful terraced gardens where the children could run, jump and play without restrictions.

I also feasted myself on the art galleries, concerts, monuments and other places of interest. One place I shall always remember—and where I myself may be remembered—is the Mellon art gallery. The day of my visit was a terribly hot one, and walking around made my feet ache so much that my shoes became unbearable. So I slipped them off and carried them under my arm. The looks on the faces of the guards were unforgettable!

And, of course, I "did" the White House, lining up for

the conducted tour of the President's home and wondering just what it was going to be like. Then it was rather disappointing, and seemed rather drab to me. Since the tour lasted for not even a quarter of an hour, I felt a bit robbed, for there had been hardly any chance to take a good look at the house. I didn't know that before too long I would live there myself and come to know every corner of that historic home!

I stayed with one family in Washington for three years. The children I took care of were lovely little tots. Virginia was like a little fairy, slender and elfin in her ways, and we used to go for long walks, taking the baby Debby in the pram. As with all children, these walks were a good opportunity to teach Virginia simple words, the names of things and so on. It is surprising what you can instill into a young boy or girl just by teaching them simple things—"this is a tree," "that is a house" and so on. Children want to learn, and even when they are tiny, you can pump a quantity of knowledge in their minds.

This is part of my job. I am not a children's teacher, but it is part of my duty, I feel, to make children aware of the world around them. A lot of nurses are content to let their children amuse themselves, but it seems to me that is taking the job only halfway. I always liked to think that any child I cared for received a good grounding of knowledge, plus good manners and a respect for his parents and other grownups. One hopes to achieve success in most cases. The way John and Caroline reacted was extremely satisfying, for everywhere I went people used to say they were a credit. Even the rest of the Kennedy family remarked that John and Caroline were somehow different from their cousins, perhaps through not having been so overindulged. You could say that this is where a nurse finds some of the joy in her work—knowing that in many ways she has left her mark on the children, and brought them up in a way that makes them likable, unspoiled and nice to know.

I returned to England in October, 1956, due to a family illness. My brother was sick, and I thought my place was with him and my sister at home in Sheerness. It was a big wrench leaving Washington and all the friends there, but I expected to return since my U.S. visa did not expire until October of the following year. Yet, after a few months at home, the idea faded. I settled down to a job as night nurse in a local hospital and was very happy there.

Even when a letter arrived in midsummer, 1957, from a good friend called Mabel Stratton, asking if I would be interested in going back to America, I had to think it over for a few days. The job available was with Mrs. Jacqueline Kennedy, wife of a Senator from Massachusetts. She was expecting a baby in December and wanted to engage an experienced nurse to look after the child. Mabel, a nurse specializing in baby care, had put my name forward, and now Mrs. Kennedy was anticipating hearing from me to say whether or not I was interested.

I left the decision for nearly a week, and then quite suddenly made up my mind to go. I wrote to Mrs. Kennedy in New York at her Park Avenue address, and a few days later she replied, asking me to telephone her on my arrival in the United States.

Even so, I very nearly did not make it. My visa was due to run out in mid-October, and when my affairs were in order in England and I was ready to book passage to New York, time was running short. Had the visa expired before arriving back in America, I would have had to undergo the whole time-wasting process of getting another one. I then found I was unable to get a booking on any ship going across the Atlantic. I practically broke into tears in the Cunard offices in London, after pleading with them to get me on the *Queen Mary*, the last ship arriving in New York before my entry visa ran out. My pleading must have moved the booking clerk, for somehow he managed to find me a berth on the huge liner.

I arrived back in America for the start of the most wonderful years of my life on October 15, 1957, just one day before the entry visa expired!

# Chapter Six

❀

❀ ❀

I MET John F. Kennedy for the first time at New York Hospital when he went to pick up baby Caroline, just eleven days old. Mrs. Kennedy had asked me to go along to help take the baby home, but I was hardly needed. Senator Kennedy took the baby himself and held her throughout the car journey back to the apartment on Park Avenue.

It was my first day with the Kennedys. On landing in New York six weeks before, I had telephoned Mrs. Kennedy and gone to meet her. At our first meeting she was very charming, and I was immediately impressed with her almost Mediterranean looks, the wide-set eyes with their deep brown coloring. It was not surprising to learn that she was of French descent. She explained that she wanted an experienced nurse for her child, and that she admired the way the English brought up their children; she herself had had an English nannie in her childhood days. Her husband, too, she said, liked the English way of doing things, since he had lived there just before the war. I said that I hoped she would like the way I did things, adding that I had always liked being with American families and had got on well with those I had worked for.

We took afternoon tea together—whether for my sake or not, I do not know—and after about an hour, Mrs. Kennedy confirmed that she would be very happy for me to work for her. We agreed that I would start on December 1, about the time her baby was expected. I had wondered why Mrs. Kennedy was in New York awaiting the birth, and it was explained that she was taking every precaution to be close to New York Hospital.

Sure enough, Caroline did come along a little early, and by that time I was on a temporary job in Washington. Mrs. Kennedy's mother, Mrs. Auchincloss, wrote to me in Washington that the baby had been born, and suggested I return to New York quickly. I did so, and joined the Kennedys the day Caroline was due to leave the hospital.

The Senator—I always called him "Senator" in those days rather than Mr. Kennedy, because I always think that if a person has a title, one ought to use it—and his wife were highly delighted with the baby. She was extra special to them because of the loss of an earlier baby.

The Senator was not often to be seen in those early New York days, being extremely busy with the Senate election campaign. Quite unversed in American politics, I had no idea of his position, potential or destiny.

I used to take the little one in to Mrs. Kennedy in the mornings when I had changed and bathed her. Her mother would sit up in bed and feed Caroline from the bottle of prepared formula, and they made a splendid picture. Once the Senator had a try at feeding the baby, but I fear the whole process was too slow for him, and after about ten minutes he handed her back to me with a smile.

"I guess this is your department after all," he said. "I had better leave it to you."

I was glad of the time we spent in New York, for it gave Mrs. Kennedy and me a chance to get to know each other's ways before the family moved to Washington. One thing did impress me tremendously about her: all the time she was in bed, she never asked me to do a single thing for her personally. It was not simply because she is an independent person, but because she never likes to put other people out, even the tiniest bit. In fact, through the seven and a half years I was with her and the children, she never asked me to as much as pick up a pin for her. Even in the White House, she never once asked me to do anything that was not strictly within my province.

One of our frequent visitors in the apartment was Mrs. Kennedy's sister, now Princess Lee Radziwill. Oddly enough, the sisters were completely different in character. Lee was outgoing, unreserved and friendly, while

Jacqueline was always a little reserved and withdrawn. It took time before she was completely friendly with me, even though I saw her every day and was entrusted to look after her children. It is not that she is the least bit unfriendly by nature—just shy. One might expect a person like her to be absolutely confident in any situation, but Mrs. Kennedy was often nervous and tense before some big occasion. I remember when Mr. Kennedy was still a Senator, she had to appear with him on television, and she was as nervous as a kitten about it. It showed up, too, on the screen, but I think it only added to her natural likability.

This inherent shyness has been passed on to Caroline, too, and, like her mother, she needs to be given confidence. She thrives on any quiet encouragement, such as the time when she was unable to ride her new two-wheeled bike. What made it awful for her was that one of her cousins, six months younger than she, could ride perfectly well. Caroline would never even try to ride the bike as long as this little chap was about. One day I took her to one side and urged her to make an effort at it. "You've nearly ridden it twice already," I said. Within half an hour she had the machine under control. Thereafter she sailed along as if she had been born on the bike.

Caroline was only four months old when we moved to Washington. The Kennedys had bought a lovely old red brick house in the Georgetown district of the capital—3307 N Street. This section always reminded me of the

Chelsea district of London, with its high narrow houses and colorfully painted doors. Mrs. Kennedy had redesigned the interior of the house, and the final decorations were supervised for her by her sister while we were in New York. By the time we arrived there it was looking very lovely.

Apart from myself, the staff comprised a butler-valet for Senator Kennedy, a cook and a housemaid. On the ground floor of the house were the reception and dining rooms, kitchen and pantry, while on the second floor was a guest room with bathroom, another bedroom and Senator and Mrs. Kennedy's double bedroom suite with bathrooms. Caroline and I had the third floor to ourselves, and very beautiful it was, too.

Apart from its splendid view of the city and the sunshine which used to stream into it, the suite was most attractively decorated. The Kennedys were delighted with their lovely daughter, and Mrs. Kennedy had seen to it that the "pink for a girl" decor was tastefully introduced.

Caroline's room had pale pink walls with a dado of little bunches of red roses. The ceiling was white, and white frilly organdy curtains were draped across the two large windows. It was a large, airy room, ideal for a child, and Caroline always slept contentedly and peacefully in it. Her crib, or rather bassinet, was decorated with two huge pink satin bows at either end and was trimmed with white and pink organdy ruffles. Her furni-

*61*

ture was white with an embossed design of pink leaves, and it stood most attractively on the soft, white carpet. Next to this room was a pink bathroom, and on the other side, with a connecting door, was my bedroom, decorated in a deep pink with white trimmings.

It was all very restful, and it got so warm in the sun that for the first five months it was quite unnecessary to take Caroline out very often. She was very serene at all times, took her bottle well, and I was able to place her quite confidently in front of one of the windows for a sun bath.

Caroline, in fact, did not have a day's illness until she was getting on to seven years old, when she had an attack of chicken pox. She also suffered a setback in her progress after being told of her father's death, but otherwise she was always a terribly contented and an easily manageable child—a sheer delight to look after. John, on the other hand, became as restless as his father had been.

Everyone settled down easily in the house, and every afternoon Mrs. Kennedy came upstairs to play with the baby. They were very pleasant afternoons; with the sun streaming in on us, we chatted about the child's progress and nibbled *petit beurre* biscuits with our English-style afternoon tea.

Senator Kennedy was extremely busy at his office in town most days and, of course, was getting tied up with the first phases of the Presidential campaign. However, I used to keep Caroline awake until about seven P.M., and he used to manage to look in at his daughter most evenings. He was delighted to be rewarded with her first smile when she was about four months old. She was lying on her tummy and just lifted her head to turn and smile at him.

It was at this time, in early 1960, that I first became aware of the importance of what the Senator was doing, for he threw himself unsparingly into the race to be nominated as Democratic candidate for the Presidency. He worked himself unmercifully for weeks on end, and on the occasions when I did see him, I noticed he was pale and looking terribly tired. While he was fighting his campaign, he rarely seemed to eat properly, contenting himself with a snack when he came home. At these times, Mrs. Kennedy herself would get up in the middle of the night and prepare him some soup or a quick meal. (His favorite was always thick tomato soup with great dollops of cream in it.) Yet no matter how tired he was, how terribly overworked, he always found time for that look in at the nursery and quick peek at Caroline, and to have a word with me about his daughter's progress.

He worked so hard, in fact, that it began to worry his family, and Mrs. Rose Kennedy, his mother, once talked to me about it, commenting that her son looked almost ill with fatigue.

"He has no need to work at all," she sighed. "And yet he never stops from one day to the next." It was true, of course. None of the Kennedys need ever have done a day's work, and they could easily have lived the life of the idle rich. However, all of them seemed gifted with the strength and stamina to do enormous amounts of work; they wanted it that way.

We were all staying at the Kennedys' Hyannis Port house that summer when the Senator got the nomination at the Los Angeles Democratic Convention, and it was a time of great excitement for the whole Kennedy clan. All the bigger children were walking around with campaign buttons about a foot wide and paper hats with "I Like Jack" or "Kennedy" on them.

But the greatest thrill of all for me came when Senator Kennedy was carried shoulder-high in a torchlight parade from Hyannis Airport to his father's house by his home-state supporters. They put on a wonderful show for him, with bands and torch flares and everyone shouting and cheering as he rode along. Caroline and I watched the procession winding up the road, with the bands playing Irish marches and everyone waving flags, and the little girl's eyes were wide with delight as she saw and heard it all happening. The house was completely flood-lit, and the whole family waited at the front for the parade to reach there. Then they joined in with a great deal of shouting and yelling and cries of congratulation. It was most moving, really, to see how Senator Kennedy was almost in tears with the emotion of the moment.

I took Caroline down to the porch and told her: "Go

and meet Daddy and give him a big kiss"—not that I needed to tell her, though. It was like unleashing her, for she shot across the path and threw herself at her father, who picked her up and gave her a huge hug and a kiss, amid the cheers and laughter of his retinue.

Senator Kennedy always loved to show his family off to his friends and supporters. I remember one time back in N Street, when he entertained a delegation of women in the house and asked me to bring Caroline down to meet them. They were all completely charmed by this lovely little girl, and when the delegation had gone, Senator Kennedy brought Caroline back to the nursery.

"Miss Shaw," he said laughingly, "Caroline is a great hit with everyone. I think she could be the greatest vote-getter of all!"

But Senator Kennedy had to make many of the campaign appearances on his own, for Mrs. Kennedy was quite unable to rush around with him all the time. She was expecting John at the time, and the pace at which her husband moved would have exhausted her. Even so, she was always up to see him off on his trips, and never failed to get up and greet him on his return. One day, after waving him off very early in the morning, she came straight to the nursery and stretched wearily in a chair while I got Caroline dressed.

"You know, Miss Shaw, it would absolutely kill me to try and keep up with my husband," she said. "Even I don't know how he keeps going day after day."

*65*

I used to say that I wished I had a vote in America, so that I could have helped him realize the goal he worked so desperately hard for.

We always stayed in Washington until about the first week in July, when we would go to the seaside house which the Kennedys had had for some time at Hyannis Port. While he was still a senator, we would usually stay there from July until the first week in December, when we would go to Palm Beach to holiday for a month with Mr. Joseph Kennedy at his beautiful home with sweeping gardens on North Ocean Boulevard. Then it was back again to the Georgetown house with its tiny garden but slightly more settled atmosphere.

As can well be imagined, baby Caroline had a profusion of lovely toys and, as with most children, she soon developed a favorite. This was a Raggedy-Ann doll with fierce red hair and pop-eyes, which we called Raggedy-Annie. This was the one who always went to bed with her. Later, on his return from a visit to Canada, President Kennedy gave her a huge replica of Annie, as tall as Caroline herself, which had been presented by some Canadian well-wishers. Caroline decided to call this one "Mother Annie." Another favorite toy was a gray donkey on wheels, and she kept that until baby John took a determined fancy to it and Caroline was persuaded, somewhat reluctantly, to give up "Neddy" to her brother.

Somehow, in our third-floor suite, Caroline and I were able to stay peacefully isolated during the Presidential election year, though I don't quite know how. By this time Caroline was going downstairs with me for breakfast, and with so many people coming and going, we got a glimpse of the terrific goings-on, the pressures and the bustle. Otherwise we went for peaceful walks and tried to keep out of the way.

Mrs. Kennedy, of course, could not be as active as she would have wished because she was expecting her second baby. I admired her tremendously for the way she carried on as best she could, helping her husband right through to Election Day and even after his election. The strain could not fail to make her tired, but nevertheless she was always ready to get up at the crack of dawn to receive breakfast visitors. She was just as ready to be at her husband's side for late-night functions, and I really don't know how, while expecting a baby, she stood up to so much constant pressure from outside.

# Chapter Seven

❀

❀   ❀

Little caroline was the first person to confirm
to Senator Kennedy that he was, in fact, President Kennedy, and I think I shall always remember with pride
how it came about—and his quiet, simple reaction to the
news that realized his greatest hope.

It happened the morning after America had gone to
the polls to choose between John F. Kennedy and Richard Nixon for the Presidency. At about seven-fifteen that
morning, Caroline woke me in my room in the Kennedy
home in Hyannis Port, and, after I had given her a quick
breakfast, she asked to go and see her Daddy in his
room.

It was a sunny morning. The November day was bright
and warm, and I awoke with a feeling of intense excitement. I had gone to bed shortly before one in the morning after listening to the election results coming in on
television. The voting was so close that no one expected a

final result before breakfasttime, and while I prepared Caroline's cornflakes and eggs, I was wondering what the outcome would be.

Caroline and I had breakfast together in her room. She was as happy and cheerful as ever, not quite realizing how important this day was to her father, of course. I got up from the table, waiting for Caroline to finish her meal, and walked across to the window.

And then, on the lawn outside the front of the house, I noticed a man in a dark suit, just standing there. He wasn't going anywhere; he just kept looking around rather carefully, taking an occasional glance toward the house. Who could it possibly be standing out on the lawn? He certainly was not one of Mr. Kennedy's aides who had been with him through the election campaign. And then I realized. He was a Secret Service man! The President's bodyguard.

I realized then that Senator Kennedy must have won.

Caroline came over to the window then and asked who the man was.

"He's a friend of your Daddy's," I told her.

She nodded, unconcerned. "May I go and see Daddy now?"

"Yes, right away," I said. "But when you go and wake him up, I want you to give him a nice surprise. Will you go in to him and say 'Good morning, Mr. President' this time?"

Caroline nodded eagerly. It seemed a good game to her.

"Will he like that?" she asked.

"Yes, I think he'll be very pleased," I said. I took her hand and led her along the corridor to Senator Kennedy's room, knocked gently on the door, opened it and let Caroline in.

The new President was just a hump in the bedclothes, but Caroline shot across the room, jumped on the bed and pulled the blankets from her father's tousled head. He grunted, opened his eyes and smiled at his daughter.

Caroline played her part perfectly and with good timing.

She said nothing until he had given her a hug and a kiss.

"Good morning, Mr. President," she said, her eyes shining with delight.

"Well now, is that right?" Caroline looked over to where I stood in the doorway, and her father's glance followed hers.

"Am I in, Miss Shaw?" he asked.

"Of course you are, Mr. President," I said.

He looked at his watch a bit doubtfully. "Well, I wasn't in the White House for sure at four-thirty this morning."

"Oh, I'm sure you've been elected, sir," I said.

He sat up in bed then and looked almost sternly at me. "Now, you just go back to the television set," he said, "and wait there until the result is confirmed, and then come back and tell me the final figures."

"Yes, sir," I said.

I hurried back to the nursery and switched on the big TV set. I switched from channel to channel, where all the newscasters were giving the latest results. According to their figures it was neck and neck, and the whole election would be decided on the result from California, Nixon's home state.

Within five minutes the result was through, and the election of the President could be definitely confirmed. I jotted down the figures and fairly skipped back to Mr. Kennedy's room. When I burst in he was playing and talking to Caroline, apparently quite calm and unconcerned.

I felt tears of happiness pricking my eyes as I stopped a few paces inside the room.

"Mr. President," I said, "you have been elected."

I read out the figures, showing that he had won. You could see the deep pleasure in his face, puffish around the eyes but still boyish and worry-free, despite the enormous burden of the campaign and the fact that he had had only four hours' sleep.

He just nodded slowly and said quietly: "Well, there we are then."

This was very typical of the man. Even though this was the summit of his ambitions, he took it all calmly. No doubt his serene reaction to being finally elected was partly due to the sheer exhaustion of the Presidential campaign, for he never seemed to be at home during all those hectic weeks, and when I did see him during that time his face looked pale with fatigue.

I don't think I ever saw him lose his temper through-out the five years I knew him. Even when something made him angry, he would listen quietly to an explana-tion and, if it was reasonable, would accept it and drop the subject. I remember this happening one time when we had moved into the White House and he complained to me about the children making too much noise and upset-ting some important State visitors. What had happened was that during the visit of Ben Bella, the then-President of Algeria, to the White House, Caroline's school had been let out to play on the White House roof during re-cess. I don't know quite how this was allowed, but any-way the children made quite a noise, it seems, while Ben Bella was making a speech on the lawns down below.

It all caused a bit of a stir in the White House, and although, naturally, the President did not tell me about it, he did ask me that evening to keep the children out of the way the next day, when Marshal Tito of Yugoslavia was due to make a speech on the White House lawn.

That morning Caroline went off to school, and I gath-ered that the teachers had been told not to let the children out during recess. So I had only little John to worry about. Of course, while all the preparations were going on down on the lawn, he wanted to go out on the Truman Balcony and have a look. I didn't think there was any harm in it, so I let him out. He loved that, staring at the men putting the platforms and microphones in place and watching the television and film cameras being lined up.

*73*

He was dressed up with a couple of six-shooters in his belt and was having a fine old time. Then one of his toy guns fell out of his belt, clattered onto the balcony and dropped through the railings down among the technicians below. I did not think any more about it, and about a quarter of an hour before the ceremony was due to start, I thought my best plan was to take John away from the White House. So I called up the Secret Service detail and asked them to fetch a car round for us. Ten minutes later we were on our way to Dumbarton Oaks for a walk in the gardens there.

But that evening I was horrified to learn that the little incident of John dropping his gun had been caught by one of the film cameras down below and inserted into a newsreel of the Tito speech, making it appear that John had been up on the balcony playing about throughout the ceremony. All the newspapers made a big thing of it, saying John had dropped his gun on Tito's head. The following morning, the President called me into his office after Caroline had gone up to school.

"Miss Shaw," he began. "I thought I asked you to keep John-John out of sight yesterday."

"Yes, you did, Mr. President," I said. "And I did take him away from the White House during the ceremony. I assure you we were at Dumbarton Oaks when he was supposed to be dropping his gun on President Tito's head."

"Is that right?" he said in surprise.

"Yes, Mr. President. You can check with the Secret Service detail."

74

He nodded. Then smiled. "All right, then. Thank you."

And that was the end of the affair. He retained this charm and coolness in spite of everything, even when, as Senator Kennedy, he was fighting bitterly to become President of the United States, and was forever traveling, talking, speechmaking and handshaking.

There was always pressure on him, and he could not escape it when he had become President-elect and had gone away on his own for a rest at his father's home in Palm Beach.

Mrs. Kennedy had stayed behind with Caroline and myself at 3307 N Street, and the President-elect was scarcely gone for an hour or so when the strain of the campaign started to have its effect on his wife. For it was then that she called up to me from her bedroom on the second floor.

"Can you come quickly, Miss Shaw?"

I knew it had started, that it was time for a trip to the hospital to have the baby.

# Chapter Eight

THE WIFE of the President-elect of the United States was, indeed, starting to have the baby. Thankfully, the doctor arrived within fifteen minutes, and almost before we could turn round, Mrs. Kennedy was on her way to Georgetown University Hospital.

It was about nine-forty-five P.M. when she first called me, and at this time President-elect Kennedy's private plane was landing or about to land near Palm Beach. Frantic messages were flashed to the aircraft, and the President was on his way home before his feet had barely touched the ground.

The arrival of the baby was quite unexpected then. It was not due until about the end of December and was, therefore, a month premature. It was November 25, 1960, when John was born—less than two hours after his mother had first called me down with the startling announcement about his pending arrival.

But the baby's early birth was really hardly surprising. The preceding weeks had been hectic in the extreme, from cheering crowds gathering outside the Hyannis Port house to greet his election along with brass bands, torchlight processions, fireworks and every other kind of jubilant activity. The President sailed through it all with his customary charm, smile and boundless energy. Mrs. Kennedy, I could tell, had been starting to feel the strain, and must have been glad to get back to Washington and have a few peaceful days to prepare for her husband's inauguration—not to speak of the baby's birth.

John's arrival by Cesarean section was followed by five days for him in an incubator, due to some minor respiratory complaint and the fact that he was a month early. It was not until he was nearly due to come out of the incubator that I saw him for the first time, and I must say he was the tiniest and sweetest little mite.

I had tried to prepare Caroline in the best way I knew possible for the arrival of a brother, and the fact that he was born so close to her own birthday was a godsend. I told her that she was going to have a little baby brother or sister for a birthday present, and she always thought for a long time after that that he sort of belonged to her. She was very fond of him and loved to do little things for him, including feeding him water from his bottle when he was just over three months old, a thing which quite shocked my friend Mabel, who worked as a nannie for the Auchincloss family.

As soon as John was a day or two old, I took Caroline

out to get him a present. We bought a lovely little silver brush and comb set, which she ever afterward insisted should be used on him.

Looking back now on the sudden arrival of John, I still think my most vivid recollection of Mrs. Kennedy is of the cool and sensible way she dealt with the emergency. Her independence asserted itself in many ways, both as the President's wife and after his death, as will be seen.

John never lived at No. 3307, for as soon as he and his mother were able to leave the hospital they went to Palm Beach, to the home of Mr. Joseph Kennedy. For those early days Mrs. Kennedy decided, quite rightly, that the little baby ought to have his own nurse for a few months, to enable me to give adequate attention to Caroline, and I suggested she might engage an old friend of mine, Mrs. Elsie Phillips. In her late fifties, Mrs. Phillips, a widow, had had many years of experience in dealing with very young babies, and she certainly was most capable during the three months she stayed. Tragically, shortly after she left, she was taken ill and died quite suddenly.

The idea of going to Palm Beach was, I think, to give Mrs. Kennedy a chance to make a proper recovery. The previous year had been so hectic, and, despite her resourcefulness, I thought that after the baby's birth she looked rather peaked.

At that time Palm Beach was at its loveliest, with wonderful sunshine. Everything on Mr. Kennedy's estate was so perfect, and Mrs. Kennedy quickly recovered in these ideal conditions. In fact, when she left for the President's inaugural ceremony in January, she looked the absolute picture of health, and it was not long before she was organizing the White House for her family's occupation.

As many people may know, she has an absolute genius for interior decoration, and by the time we were ready to move from Palm Beach to the White House, in late February, 1961, she had achieved great changes in the second-floor apartments where we were to live for the next two years and nine months.

We had not seen much of the President-elect up to the time of his inauguration, although he joined his family at Palm Beach for Christmas and spent as much time as possible with his children. After his inauguration we saw even less of him until we moved into the White House. But I do know that he was absolutely delighted with the way his wife had transformed the place into a home suitable for the children as well as for themselves and the powerful and influential guests who were bound to visit.

The principal feature of the apartments was a large central corridor, used as a sitting room, off which were situated the bedrooms, bathrooms, etc., the famous Lincoln bedroom with its original furniture and the huge oval reception room, which was used for only the more formal receptions. It was really too large to be for family sitting.

At one end of the corridor a passage led to a bedroom and sitting room that had formerly been used by Margaret Truman, and these were turned into a dining room with a kitchen adjoining, which was an absolute boon for the serving of piping hot food. In the past, apparently, the food had to be taken up on the lifts and then wheeled along the corridor before being served; it had sometimes been served unpalatably cold.

The kitchen next to the dining room was therefore a great acquisition, and the chef was able to use it without the risk of upsetting anyone with cold food. The children's meals were always nice and hot and, more important as far as they were concerned, always absolutely freshly cooked.

The dining room had another wonderful attribute, thanks to Mrs. Kennedy, which was a great help to me in entertaining first Caroline and then, as he grew older, John. It was covered with the most fascinating wallpaper.

This paper had been carefully peeled off the walls of a house being demolished—Mrs. Kennedy had heard about it somehow, how I don't know—and the paper had been brought to the White House and replastered onto the walls in the dining room. The feature of it was that it depicted great historic moments in American battle history, including scenes of the British Redcoats in the War of Independence. Where the paper was slightly torn or disfigured, Mrs. Kennedy had brought in a very clever artist to restore it perfectly. It fascinated the children, and they were kept occupied for hours, studying the different soldiers in the bright-colored uniforms. They kept asking: "What's he doing?" or "Why is he like that?"

They were curious about the Redcoats one day, and when I tried to explain what had happened to them, the President joked about it and said: "It's tough on you Miss Shaw, an Englishwoman, having to talk about the outcome of *that* battle." However, I think I managed to sort out the battle for the children without too much honor being lost on my side!

The children's rooms were on either side of mine, right in the center of the White House, over the pillared portico and looking out on the sweeping lawns and gardens at the front. They were in an ideal location, except perhaps they did not always catch the sun, and they were used by me and the children on numerous occasions as the perfect lookout for Presidential receptions in front of the building and for seeing many other ceremonial occasions.

As before, Caroline's room was decorated in pink and white, but this time she had a canopy bed and a window seat covered with pink brocade. It really was an enormous room, and for several months the little girl was slightly in awe of it at night. There was plenty of space for her dozens of toys, just about everything any child could wish for. It was just as well she did have so much room, for there were toys in abundance, among them a really beautiful, large doll house, which had been given to her by Madame de Gaulle on her state visit with the President of France.

The profusion of toys for both Caroline and John was rather a problem for their parents, because they kept ar-

20. Watching from behind the shrubbery, Mrs. Kennedy and John observe formal ceremonies on the south grounds of the White House, honoring Ahmed Ben Bella, former premier of Algeria. I have less courage and am caught peeking over the top.

21. A morning ride in Virginia. Mrs. Kennedy and John are on Sardar, a purebred Arabian given to her by President Ayub Khan of Pakistan, and Caroline again on Macaroni.

*Howard Allen from Underwood & Underwood*

*Cecil W. Stoughton*

22. The Truman balcony at the White House. This was the vantage point from which the children and I watched all the comings and goings.

*Cecil W. St*

23. A charming snapshot, one of my favorites, of the President and his family in Palm Beach.

Mrs. Kennedy takes
o-year-old John to meet Major
rdon Cooper after ceremonies
noring the astronaut's 22-orbit
p around the earth.

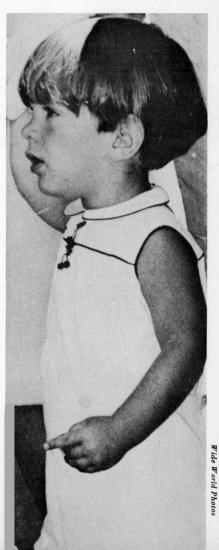

25. There was a bit of a
ruckus over the length of John's
hair, until it was cut by a
jocular "Presidential order."

26. & 27. If I had to choose two pictures summing up my life with John, they would be these. Watching the helicopter land on the White House lawn was a passion of his, and we had only to learn of its arrival to dash out of the house to look. But when it left with the President aboard, we usually had tears—not so much because his father was going off, but because he was not allowed to go on the "chopper."

Retreat.

Welcome home.

30. August, 1963.
The President and Caroline visit Mrs. Kennedy, who is resting at the Otis Air Force Base hospital after the loss of her son Patrick.

*Wide World Photos*

31. John looks at a puppy eye-to-eye.

Pals.

33. Mrs. Kennedy and John
on their way to church. This is the
first time the whole family
worshiped together in public.

34. Plane trips were exciting for both the children. The crew would play games with them and lay out extra sweets—always a great adventure.

35. The President looks a bit bemused by these Halloween ghouls.

riving at the White House from every conceivable direction. In the end, the President decided that only presents given by the closest friends and relations should be accepted by the children, and the rest were channeled into the Kennedy Foundation Hospital for Children.

The doll house from Madame de Gaulle kept Caroline occupied for hours, along with her toy poodle, which we called Tinkerbelle, and the many dolls of all shapes, colors and sizes. Not that she spent very much time indoors, for I am a great believer in the outdoor life, and whenever possible we would get out into the White House grounds or to Montrose Park, where I would meet the other nannies, nurses or governesses with their charges, and where the children would play games quite happily as we chatted while keeping them under close surveillance.

John's room was, of course, blue and white, and was also extremely large. It had a two-ring gas stove on which I could prepare his formula and solids, and the same very attractive crib that Caroline had used but with the pink bows exchanged for blue ones.

Although John made quite good progress at Palm Beach under Mrs. Phillips, he was not doing as well as I would have liked, and when we left for the White House, I still thought he was a little underweight and not as contented as he ought to have been. I don't think there was any particular reason for this, but for some weeks he did have restless periods, particularly in the afternoons, when he cried a lot. In the end, I decided to switch his diet. Instead of letting him have his beef extract in the late morning or evening, I gave it to him at lunchtime, and, whenever he would take it down, I made him eat as much of his formula as possible, sometimes increasing or decreasing the strength of it as required.

After a few weeks of this he slept better in the afternoons and started to put on weight. I was very gratified about this, particularly when next Mr. Joseph Kennedy saw the little chap, after a break of a few weeks. He said: "My word, Miss Shaw, what have you been doing to him? He looks twice the fellow he was. He's really doing well now."

Going into the White House was, for me, a formidable experience. I had told Caroline that we were moving to a bigger house because there was not enough room in No. 3307 for us all. She was very pleased with the idea and even more delighted when she saw her new home, because, as she said, there was so much room in which to play and "a great big garden, too."

Personally, I didn't get over my awe at living in the White House for quite a long time. I had seen it only once previously, on a ten-minute tour, and to be walking in through the imposing portals was an inspiring moment.

The ground floor was full of large pictures of previous Presidents and their wives, and there seemed to be staff of one kind or another almost everywhere, from Secret Service agents to butlers, maids, houseboys and servants of every type and kind. In addition, there were White

House officials, chauffeurs, sentries, policemen and many people going in and out on official business.

Only after we had taken the smoothly operated elevator to the second floor did I feel that we were "away from it all" in our own little kingdom. Yet even then there were more servants around than I had ever believed possible. While this initially appeared to be rather overwhelming, the profusion of willing helpers had its advantages, particularly when Caroline got a little older and had the urge to wander off and explore a little on her own. I thought it was natural for a child of her intelligence and high I.Q. to want to discover the ways and workings of the place, and I had some good allies among the staff in helping to keep an eye on her.

Incidentally, one of the most impressive things about the place was the wonderful politeness and willingness to help shown by every member of the White House, from Mr. West, the chief usher, to the lowliest housemaid. Every one of the staff seemed to go out of his or her way to be kind, and nothing was too much trouble. I remember on one occasion ringing down to the office that handled all the requests for assistance of any kind and, after saying what I wanted, apologizing for causing any trouble. Came the pleasant response: "Don't worry, Miss Shaw, you are no trouble to us at all." Of course, I realize that the answer lay in the children, who had really captivated the staff. I don't think any request made by them or on their behalf would have been too much trouble. They were absolutely idolized.

After we had been in the White House for about four months, the President and Mrs. Kennedy were anxious to get Caroline into kindergarten. Various schemes were considered. Already a group of parents friendly with the Kennedys had started play-mornings, in which their children got together in one or another of their parents' homes and enjoyed games and toys while the mothers or nannies had a cup of coffee. Of course the children loved these times, but they were not really learning anything more than how to appreciate each other's company.

The idea of setting up a school somewhere had been discussed, and it was suggested to Mrs. Kennedy that it would be possible to have the school in the White House itself. The idea seemed to be attractive, and in her enthusiastic and well-organized way, Mrs. Kennedy soon had the kindergarten school set up in the third-floor solarium, which President Eisenhower had used in his White House days for relaxation and catching the sun. Desks for each child were brought in, toilet facilities installed and the usual accouterments of a nursery school or kindergarten were prepared. The school accommodated between a dozen and fifteen children during the school year, all about three and a half to four and a half, and all coming from family friends of the Kennedys or the embassies in Washington. It was a great success, and I'm pleased to be able to report that Caroline was among the brightest pupils.

After the President's assassination the school in the White House had to close rather abruptly but still carried on in the British Embassy at the insistence of the wife of the British Ambassador, Mrs. Ormsby-Gore, soon to become Lady Harlech.

While Caroline was starting school, John was developing rapidly and seemed to thrive in the wonderful home. We established a set routine for the children, despite all the comings and goings of the President and Mrs. Kennedy, who were both extremely busy on official duties. It was a routine which they settled into beautifully. But despite its normalcy, it had its hectic moments quite unexpectedly.

# Chapter Nine

❀

❀  ❀

M Y DAY in the White House began, usually, at about six A.M. In the early days, it was essential to be up and about at this time, since baby John then needed his first feed, and I used to slip into my big bathroom and prepare his bottle there, since the room was big enough to keep his bottle-warmer, formula, diapers and such essential equipment.

At around seven o'clock, Caroline would wake up and come into my room to say good morning. It was always delightful to see Caroline at that hour, all sleepy and with tousled hair. She was never too sleepy to chat, though —nothing on earth would stop Caroline from chattering! Having got John back to his crib and tucked down, I used to tell Caroline to go wash up and brush her teeth and then we'd both get dressed. I always feel it is a good thing to be doing something while a little child—Caroline was three and a half by the time we were settled into the White House—dresses itself. It demonstrates to them that you are busy, so they are more inclined to do things for themselves. At that age, Caroline was able to dress herself almost completely, including doing up her shoes.

Between seven-thirty and eight, the two of us sat down to breakfast in the little dinette. Caroline always had a good breakfast of cereal, eggs and bacon and things like that, since she always had a light lunch. I much preferred eating on our own in the dinette, because I was able to organize things much better by myself than if we had eaten in one of the large dining rooms.

Neither of the children was any bother when it came to eating. They both ate everything that was put in front of them—although just occasionally John would have to be coaxed when he decided he did not want to eat something or other. The rest of the Kennedy family always used to remark on the way both Caroline and John ate their meals up without fuss, and the cook down at the Palm Beach house was always delighted to have my two—"It does me good to see them clean their plates," she would say.

I used to have a rule with them when they each began to take proper meals. If there was something on the plate that they did not much like the look of, I used to say to them: "Now, you just try one spoonful. If you really don't like it, leave the rest. But the next time you have it, try two spoonfuls." We used to do this, and sure enough, the day would come when they would eat up their spinach or whatever it was without a murmur.

*90*

This one-spoonful, two-spoonful routine went down well with the children. I'll never forget one time when Sydney Lawford came to dinner and found something on her plate she did not care for too much. I think it actually was spinach this time. Anyway, when Sydney turned up her nose at it and said something to Caroline, I heard Caroline tell her quite sharply: "Now, Sydney, you must try one spoonful. If you don't like it, you are allowed to leave the rest. But next time, you must try two spoonfuls. You'll like it in the end. That's how I got to like spinach."

The tempo of our meals was always gauged by the amount of talking Caroline did. Later, while John got down to eating and concentrated on that alone, Caroline would chatter away throughout the meal, telling us about her school day, what her friends said and so on. Sometimes I would have to interrupt her to make her get on with her meal, but usually I did not stop her talking, for learning to express herself was part of growing up and this process should not be stifled.

Anyway, after breakfast it was time for the children to go and see their father and mother. The President was always up at the same time and was usually to be found in the lounge or dining room of his suite just after eight-fifteen. I used to take the children down to him and leave them with him. When Caroline started going to the school in the solarium, the President used to take her downstairs to his office and wait there with her until she could join all her school friends after they had assembled on the lawn outside his window.

From there on, John was the only one to worry about until midday, when school was over for Caroline. When he was tiny, I used to spend an hour or so bathing him, changing his clothes and preparing his formula, and then Mrs. Kennedy would come into the nursery to help feed him. She used to love doing simple things like that, since life was usually so hectic for her in the White House that such hours she could spend with her children were very precious to her.

On the other hand, she was content to let me have full charge of the children and bring them up the way I felt sure she wanted me to do. It was very pleasing to me—and something I am very proud of—that both the President and Mrs. Kennedy always left it to me to do what I thought best for their children. I appreciated their trust greatly.

Soon after we moved into the White House she demonstrated her faith in me, when I had a small difference of opinion with one of the chefs about the kind of menu the children ought to have. I had asked the chefs if I could prepare a menu for them to follow which covered a three-week period, and which would give the children something different at every meal for three weeks. It is a bit difficult to vary meals like that, but after a bit of juggling and working out, it can be done. However, the chefs said this was not necessary, and that they would see to it themselves. Well, I did not want to make a nuisance of myself, so I said no more and let them try.

During the second week, when we had had liver served

up for dinner for the third time in four days, I decided to tackle the chefs again. It was no good going on like this, because I saw Caroline's nose turn up as that meal was served to her.

"Liver!" she said. "Miss Shaw, why do we have to have liver again?"

"Oh, I expect the cooks made a mistake tonight," I said. "Anyway, you like liver. Come along, show me you can eat it all up."

Good little character that she was, Caroline ate it up without complaining, but I resolved to go down to the kitchens in the morning and do a bit of complaining myself. After all, to make children eat properly, you have to take care that their meals are interesting, varied and colorful, and even if they are fond of a particular meal, you can't give it to them too often or they will quickly tire of it.

So the next morning, I went to the kitchen to do battle with the chefs, three of whom were working there at the time. The head chef was a charming Frenchman, and assisting him were an Italian chef and a Filipino cook. I was greeted by the Italian, and when I told him that I would like him to follow my menu, he simply shrugged and said that there was no need.

"But you have sent us liver three time in four days," I persisted. "I really think you ought to be guided by me."

Just then, a soft voice behind me said: "Quite right, Miss Shaw."

I turned and found Mrs. Kennedy standing there, apparently having heard everything that had been said, for she stepped past me and quite clearly told the chef that in the future he would follow the menu I had prepared without question or alteration. I felt a bit embarrassed at having brought Mrs. Kennedy into the discussion, albeit unwittingly, but I was glad, too, for it put an end to liver for a few weeks!

After that, we kept to our strictly balanced and assorted diet. I was happy about it for the children's sake and also my own, since I ate an evening meal with them as a matter of convenience to myself and the chefs.

During the mornings in the White House, Mrs. Kennedy used to come to the nursery as often as she was able. She would sit and talk while little John was fast asleep in his pram on the Truman Balcony—the second-floor balcony which President Truman had added to the White House.

Incidentally, I was told that he got into hot water for having it added to the White House, for many people thought it did not go with the rest of the construction, although it always seemed perfectly fitting to me. The balcony was ideal, not only as a place to park John when he was a baby but also as a vantage point from which the children could watch the comings and goings of important people. I once met President Truman when he was visiting the Kennedys on one of their informal, off-duty evenings, and told him how much his balcony was appreciated now.

"Well, now, Miss Shaw," he said, his eyes twinkling kindly. "I sure am glad *someone* likes it."

When I talked with Mrs. Kennedy those mornings, I used to tell her everything that had been happening in the nursery. She missed so much of her children's growing up because of the tremendous pressures on her time, so she was glad to hear about them developing and to catch the little things they said to me and to each other.

In a small way, I used to try and make up for what she had missed by relating as carefully as possible all the little things—funny little events which would seem trivial and unimportant to anyone but a mother. Later on, Mrs. Kennedy said how much she used to enjoy those moments of catching up with her children.

When he got a little older and was able to walk and run, I used to take John onto the lawn to join the other children from the school at midmorning recess. John's particular chum at that time was a little boy at the school, and they always made a beeline for each other the first moment they could, and would chase and play, romping and scuffling over all the place. The playground on the lawn had all the equipment a children's kindergarten could want, including a big doll house. And it was here that poor little John lost one of his front teeth!

He was playing in and out of the house with his little friend when he took a terrific fall and banged his teeth on the corner of a step. When I suddenly heard him cry-

*95*

ing, I whirled round and saw the little chap lying there with blood coming out of his mouth. I was appalled. Yet, bless him, he never made a screaming fuss about it. After I had comforted him a little, he suddenly darted away and came back with a tooth in his hand and gave it to me! Anyway, the moment I notified the medical staff at the White House that little John had been injured, there was a tremendous to-do. I went first to the Navy doctor who looked after the White House medical affairs, but was told to go directly to Dr. Janet Travell, President Kennedy's personal doctor.

I was all for pushing the tooth back into John's gum after it had been sterilized, but we had to wait for a dentist to arrive, and when he did, he said that the tooth could not now be put back for fear of tetanus.

The President and Mrs. Kennedy were quite upset that their son would now have a gap in his front teeth, and the President tackled me about it.

"Miss Shaw," he asked me that evening, when he came to say good night to the children, "why didn't they put John's tooth back in his gum?"

I explained to him exactly what had happened and the reason why it could not be done. He listened patiently and then nodded. He was a very fair man and would never blame anyone for anything once he had been given a reasonable explanation. Anyway, that's how poor John came to walk about with a gap in his teeth for the next few years.

The President's children were both extremely healthy.

Neither suffered any serious illness, and, in fact, the first time they ever had to be confined to bed was when they caught chicken pox after moving from the White House.

Neither Caroline nor John were particularly early developers. On the contrary, they were, if anything, a little late in mastering the art of walking. Caroline, for instance, was walking well at a little over a year. On the other hand, she never went through the stage of standing up and falling down all the time. It seemed as if she made up her mind to walk only when she knew she could do it properly, and from the outset she walked well.

Neither did she spend too much time creeping about on her hands and knees. Caroline had her own way of getting about. She walked on the flats of her hands and feet, with her bottom high up in the air. It was not only cute but almost acrobatic. Anyway, she made pretty fast time that way, much to her parents' amusement.

She was the same at sitting up. Most babies go through a stage of being propped up and then slopping over when they lose support. Caroline didn't. She was a bit late in sitting herself up, but when she did manage it, she sat up and stayed up.

In comparing the early development of Caroline and John, I think John suffered a great handicap by being brought up in the White House, surrounded by all the restrictions that have to be placed on a President's children. When Caroline was first learning to get about and talk, she and I would go for quiet walks down the street, visit the drugstore together for ice creams and things like that, things that John could never do without Secret Service men trailing behind him and, unwittingly, causing a sensation.

Mrs. Kennedy used to remark rather wistfully how sad it was that her son was unable to enjoy such simple pleasures as his sister had. One of Caroline's great pleasures, for instance, had been helping me wash up and put away the lunch things, but John never got that chance, for our washing up and putting away was all done by servants at the White House.

Both the children started talking at about the same stage, and, of course, both went through the stage of asking endless questions. John was particularly wearing with his machine-gun bursts of questions about everything and anything. Caroline was always a bit more thoughtful about hers—things stuck in her mind, perhaps for weeks, and then she would ask something about an event which, for everyone else, was over and forgotten.

We did not encourage baby talk in the White House nursery. I myself do not care overmuch for children speaking baby language. It is charming and amusing sometimes to hear little tots struggling to pronounce a word, but I always think it better to try and correct them rather than let them go on thinking they have said the word properly. But it did take John quite a little while to master his sister's name. "Caroline" was too much of a mouthful for him when he was a toddler, and the nearest he could get to it was "Cannon."

Of course, babies do a whole lot of talking even before the words become intelligible. I remember the President being puzzled at John not talking when he was quite small.

"When is he going to talk, Miss Shaw?" he asked one day while we were playing with him in the nursery.

"Oh, but he does talk, Mr. President," I said. "It's just that you can't understand him."

"That's right, Daddy," put in Caroline. "He does talk to me."

The President laughed at that. "Well, I guess you'd better interpret for me," he said.

Caroline had a wonderful mother instinct which developed early with the arrival of a baby brother so soon. She used to help me feed him, tuck him down in his crib and things like that, and was always ready to scamper in to him in answer to his shrill cries of "Cannon! Cannon!" She really was a great help to me in looking after John, and she had the knack of bossing John without putting his back up.

In my White House afternoons, I was allowed to make what arrangements I liked for the children, providing Mrs. Kennedy did not have any special plans for them herself. Very often we would go over to see some of the children's friends, which increased my own circle of friends because I was made completely welcome everywhere. Often we would bring children back to dinner with Caroline and John or take them for a walk at Dumbarton Oaks. Only one thing never changed when we were out—there were always two Secret Service men along with us.

Whenever the children wanted to go out, I first had to telephone a certain number on the White House switchboard and speak to the children's Secret Service detail. There were three men assigned to John and Caroline: Mr. Lynn Meredith, the head of the detail, Mr. Bob Foster and Mr. Tom Wells. And all of them were wonderful men. I missed them very badly when Mrs. Kennedy moved to New York after the President's death. Mr. Meredith was particularly kind, for he did a great many things to help me personally, such as helping me with my driving insurance, tax forms and so forth.

They became great friends to the children, but I always insisted that Caroline and John should refer to them and speak to them as "Mister" Meredith, or "Mister" Foster. The men were a little surprised at this because, being Americans, they were very friendly, and had introduced themselves to the children as Bob or Tom. I always thought it better for the little ones to address them in the more formal manner, not only out of respect but also because it made it easier for the men to control the children if they had to tell them to do something. The agents thought it quite odd—very English, they said it was—but it was my way and they went along with it.

There were always two of them with me when I went out with the children. Whenever I called their office in the White House to tell them we were going out, they brought a big station wagon round to the back door for us, and stayed with us wherever we went until we were all safely back in the President's home. They never intruded. One hardly noticed them, but they were always there.

In the early evening, when we got back to the White House, I usually took the children to play out on the lawn or, if the weather was bad, we went to the White House cinema to see a movie. All the Kennedys were great movie fans—it was one of the President's favorite ways of relaxing on his rare evenings off—and even when he was just toddling, little John liked to be taken along with his sister and her friends.

Caroline was a very popular girl because she was never bossy or pushing. As much as anything else, she loved to amuse herself. She was an ardent reader, reading to herself very rapidly. Her father was famous for his ability to read very quickly, and Caroline had the same facility. She could skim through a book almost as quickly as I could, but still retain all the details. There was no question that she did not take in every word, for often when I was reading to her from books she had also read on her own, I might skip a word or mix up a sentence; she would immediately say: "Miss Shaw, you went wrong there."

Both she and John adored having stories read to them in bed, and I always did this for them just before they were tucked down for the night. Even if they had been naughty during the day, candies or visits out might be withheld but never their nightly read. They looked forward to it so much, and it was, after all, part of their education. In any case, I enjoyed it myself!

Caroline had quite a little library of books. When I went on vacation to England, as I did every summer, I brought her back Beatrix Potter's children's books and other simple readers. She kept her books tidily and looked after them carefully enough to be able to hand them on to John when she had progressed to more difficult books. I always tried to encourage reading, painting, drawing and other forms of self-amusement. I have found that you have to teach children concentration; it is not something they are born with. You need to sit them down with a drawing book and crayons and encourage them to draw and interest them in the colors, suggesting things they might like to sketch and so on. In this way, they gradually become interested in doing it for themselves, and they will unconsciously learn to concentrate. I used to set Caroline working by herself like this, then fetch John and help him play with a pile of colored bricks, all the time playing, but setting him little problems of balancing the bricks on top of each other until he became absorbed in it. It takes a bit of time to bring out a child's concentration, but it is time well spent.

After dinner and—on special occasions—the movies, the big time in the children's lives at the White House came when they were allowed down to their father's office on the ground floor. This used to happen at about seven-thirty or eight o'clock. I took them down, first of all, to see Mrs. Evelyn Lincoln, President Kennedy's secretary, a wonderful woman who was absolutely devoted to Mr. Kennedy, and who delighted in playing with the children. She used to let them play with her typewriter, crawl over the carpets, swing on the swivel chairs and generally do as they pleased until the President had finished his work. Then, the children went down to the huge indoor swimming pool with the President for his evening swim. He never missed this swim, for it was part of the exercises he had to do to strengthen his back, which troubled him from time to time. The children loved plunging into the pool, and it was wonderful to see them all romping and splashing about together.

It always seemed to do the President good to cast off the cares of the day and retreat into the tiny world of his children. Once again, I liked to leave them by themselves whenever I could, so that for some brief moments the children and their father were quite alone together. Mrs. Kennedy always tried, though it was often difficult for her, to get down to play with them at this time, and she often went for a swim too. If the President was delayed in getting away from his office, I swam with the children until he came down.

After the evening swim, I took the children back up to the second floor for a short play and then—bed.

I never had any trouble getting John or Caroline off to their beds. From the very beginning with both of them, bedtime was bedtime with no nonsense, and I never had to tell them twice. The secret with the children was to prepare them for bed ten minutes or a quarter of an hour before they had to go and change into their nighties. When they were playing with their toys or maybe reading, I used to go in to them and inquire what they were doing. Then, when they'd told me, I'd say: "Fine. You have ten more minutes, and then it will be time for bed."

"Yes, Miss Shaw," they would say. At the end of ten minutes I would go back, help them finish their game or let them read down to the end of a page. Then I would jolly them along to the bathroom and finally get them into their beds. I always read to them for ten minutes, said their prayers with them and tucked them down.

The President and Mrs. Kennedy usually came up to give the children their good-night kiss at prayer time. No matter who was in the White House or what was happening in the outside world, the President never failed to come up to the nursery to see his children tucked down in their beds. He would come along quietly and without fuss. Often he listened at the door for a few moments before coming in.

I was teaching the children a new prayer once— "Thank you, God, for the world so sweet"—and did not notice President Kennedy standing behind me. When I had finished, he spoke.

"That's a lovely prayer, Miss Shaw," he said. "Is it an English one?"

"Yes, Mr. President," I said.

"Well, I like it. I hope they learn it."

This was one of the things I loved about the Kennedys.

They were staunch Catholics, and I am not a Catholic, but it never seemed to worry them what prayers were said. Perhaps they felt as I do, that it is important for children to understand that there is some higher Being they can turn to, pray to, whenever they feel the need. I believe everyone needs some kind of faith to cling to, and the differences between various religions seem to me to be unimportant, as long as children do understand that there is a God to care for them and to whom they can turn.

Mrs. Kennedy was always broad-minded about this. Once I got slightly muddled between the Catholic and another version in teaching the children the Lord's Prayer. This time, she happened to be standing at the door while I said the prayer with John and Caroline.

When I had finished, Mrs. Kennedy smiled: "That's the Episcopalian version, isn't it, Miss Shaw?"

"Oh, is it?" I said. "I'm sorry . . . I forgot."

Mrs. Kennedy shrugged. "It doesn't matter."

One remarkable thing about children is the complete unawareness of any difference between themselves and colored people. The Kennedys used to have a colored manservant up at Hyannis Port named George. George was a great favorite of Caroline's in her toddler days, and he had a remarkable gift of patience with the little girl. She used to talk to him for hours on end about absolutely nothing at all, just babbling on happily while George listened and nodded and said "yes" and "no" in all the right places.

*105*

"I don't know how you do it, George," I said to him one day. "Even I can't make out what she is saying."

George just smiled: "We get along just fine, Miss," he said. "It doesn't take words to make a friend."

Anyway, Caroline never once remarked on his color until one time when we were all down at Palm Beach. Caroline noticed for the first time that she was turning brown in the hot sunshine, and then she discovered for herself that George was permanently colored.

"George," she said to him. "How did you get that color? I've been in the sun all day and I'm only a bit brown."

"Well, Miss," chuckled George, "I've been lying in the sun all my life, I guess."

After that she never asked another question about the subject.

As I say, there was never any fuss at bedtime in the White House nurseries, apart from the question of leaving Caroline's door slightly ajar. I thought at first that she wanted it open because her room was so large and so high, and knowing that this could frighten a child a bit, I did not question her. But when we had been in the White House a few months, I asked about it and got a perfectly logical explanation.

"Caroline," I said. "Why do you like the door open? You're a big girl now."

"Oh, Miss Shaw," she said. "I always feel that if you shut the door, maybe you won't be able to open it again quickly if I want you." I must say that brought a lump to my throat.

"All right, darling," I said, giving her a good-night kiss. "We'll leave it open. You know I'll come if you call."

When the children were tucked down, I used to go to my own room and read all the day's papers to keep myself in touch with the outside world, make endless telephone calls to my friends in Washington—everyone seems to spend hours on the phone there!—and then do some knitting or maybe mend one of Caroline's doll dresses. I always took a peek into their rooms to make sure the children were asleep, and then turned in myself.

It was a fairly hectic and tiring day at the White House, but that last look at Caroline and John, seeing them sleeping peacefully and contentedly, was a wonderful reward for a day's work. I was very happy there.

# Chapter Ten

❈

❈    ❈

THE SECURITY PRECAUTIONS taken for the Kennedy children at the White House—and everywhere else they went—were meticulous. As I said before, John and Caroline had three Secret Service men of their own to guard them, and any time we went out of the house, two of them would come with us, one in our car and another in a tail car. These three—Mr. Lynn Meredith, Mr. Bob Foster and Mr. Tom Wells—were most charming men. They loved the children and would do anything for them. The men were always armed and watchful with the children, but Caroline and John grew so fond of them that the Secret Service detail became like a trio of favorite uncles. One of them, Mr. Foster, for instance, taught John to ride a bike after hours of patient encouragement.

At times their devotion to the children was a bit frustrating, for whenever John wanted anything, he knew he had only to ask one of the Secret Service men for it. Caroline used to be horrified at her little brother. I remember one day I got cross with one of the men for giving John candy just before lunch.

"Why do you give him candy?" I asked. "You all know he's not supposed to have it before lunch. You really shouldn't do it."

The big, husky fellow shuffled his feet. "Well, gee, Miss Shaw, I like to give him things."

"That makes no difference," I said. "He should not have candy. Now don't give him any more."

"No, Miss Shaw," he said. But I knew he wouldn't take much notice of me—and neither would any of the others. These men would have laid down their lives for the children, so it was not likely they would refuse them candy.

Yet this devotion to the children had its drawbacks. Whatever the children wanted to do was all right by the Secret Service men, and I remember one incident while the President and his family were on holiday at their home in Hyannis Port. Like all his other residences, this house had been fenced off for privacy and guarded from the moment he had been elected. Whenever he was there, Secret Service men kept guard on all the entrances and forbade anyone to come and go without scrutiny. But they had a blind spot about the children.

This particular time, I had taken the children into the garden and was playing with John when I noticed Caroline was missing. It always made me go hot and cold when I missed them for even a moment, and I began to search the grounds a bit frantically. Then I hurried to the nearby gate to ask the Secret Service man: "Have you seen Caroline?"

He smiled. "Sure, she just went down the road."

"What!" I exploded. "You mean to say you just let her wander out of the gate and down the road?"

"Well, I didn't stop her, as I had my eye on her, ma'am," he said.

"But she's a little girl of five," I said. "Would you let any other little girl of that age run down the road like that?"

I did not wait for an answer, but dashed down the road and found Caroline calmly walking along the grass verge looking for flowers. As quietly as I could, I took her hand and led her back to the house. I had something to say to the Secret Service people after that. President's children or not, I felt the children could not be allowed to wander at will—in their own interests. After that episode, there were notices posted on all the gates, forbidding the guards to let the children out of the grounds unless they were with their own particular Secret Service detail or myself. Of course, the guards meant well, but it made me worry to think John or Caroline might just wander away whenever they felt like it.

One afternoon, the three of us, with our Secret Service men at a discreet distance, went to a neighboring house to play on the beach. We were all playing sandcastles, when I noticed a woman I had never seen before walking toward us. I glanced around, and although the Secret Service men had her in sight, I walked a few paces toward the woman and stood between her and the children. She came up to us with a pleasant smile on her face.

"Say, I hear the Kennedy children are coming down here today," she began. "Do you know when they are arriving?"

"No," I lied. "I'm afraid I don't know anything about them." The children were still absorbed in their game and hardly bothered to look up, even when the woman went to them and watched them for a moment.

"Gee, I'd sure like to see them," she said. "I guess they must be real nice kids." She patted John Kennedy on the head as she spoke, quite oblivious to who he was. She went on chatting for a moment or two more, saying she was staying nearby and would love to have a snapshot of the President's children. I sympathized with her, and she walked away again. I'm sure she was quite innocent, but if she did not know John Kennedy when she patted him on the head, that was fine by me.

I never volunteered any information to anyone about who the children were or what they were doing or going to do. Of course, John often used to spill the truth himself by thrusting out his little hand and saying proudly: "I'm John F. Kennedy, Junior."

We had scares, but the worst time, I think, was at Glen Ora when Caroline was missing for quite a while, or so it seemed to me.

She had been playing on the farm which adjoins Glen

Ora, where there were a couple of ponds, little chicken houses and so on which naturally fascinated the children. I had been playing with John for a while, looked around for Caroline and could not see her anywhere. I hunted around, called her name but she did not reply—and then I got really worried. I hurried back to the house and called the Secret Service men. Together we scoured the grounds, the house and the farmyard, but still there was no sign of Caroline. I was absolutely frantic after minutes that seemed hours, and the Secret Service men were worried too.

Then Mr. Meredith came to me and said: "Miss Shaw, we are going to have to search down by the ponds."

I held my breath for a moment as the dreadful thought passed through my mind. I was on the verge of tears. . . .

"Miss Shaw." I whirled around at the sound of Caroline's voice behind me, and I saw her climbing out of one of the little chicken houses, quite unconcerned.

That, I know, was the only time I smacked Caroline without sufficient reason. I was so frightened moments before and now so relieved that I gave her a hard smack on the bottom.

"You naughty girl," I scolded her. "Never, never hide from me again."

"But I wasn't hiding from you," she said reproachfully. "I was playing with my dollies in the little house."

I just hugged her with relief. I think Caroline was utterly bewildered with me. We comforted each other, for she could see I had been worried, and I was sorry I had smacked her.

Mrs. Kennedy never liked the Secret Service men too close to her children. When they first attached themselves to her and to us, she told them to keep as well out of the way as possible and yet be on guard, because she did not want her children to feel crowded. She wanted them always to be free. But after another scaring episode, she had to agree to let the men stay within eyesight of the children. This happened on one of my days off, when Caroline and John were taken with some friends to swim in the pool down home in Virginia. Caroline, who had no fear of the water, jumped into the pool and was swimming around, hanging onto a float. Somebody evidently thought she was way out of her depth and jumped in to fish her out, although I'm told she was in no actual danger.

I was told about the incident the next day, but it did not seem too important, since the scare was over. But two or three days afterward, Mr. Meredith, chief of the children's guard detail, called me aside.

"This thing has been picked up by the papers," he said. "It will be in the news tomorrow."

"Right," I said. "I'll go and tell Mrs. Kennedy about it and put the whole thing straight before she reads it."

I managed to catch Mrs. Kennedy that afternoon and told her the whole story, emphasizing that the newspaper

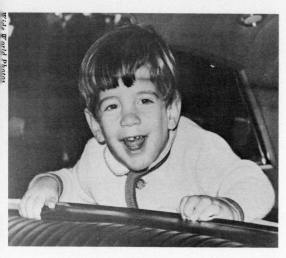

36. John was very good when he lost his front tooth and hardly cried at all. But he did go around with a bit of a gap after that.

37. The President and his family enjoyed the exhibition marching of the Black Watch Regiment on the White House lawn, and took even greater pleasure in examining their uniforms at first hand. This picture was taken just nine days before the President was assassinated.

*R. L. Knudsen*

38. No one was left unmoved by the President's death, but to me it was especially heartbreaking to see this young, strong and beautiful family left without a husband and a father.

39.  November 25, 1963. John salutes his father's casket outside St. Matthew's Cathedral.

40.  Mrs. Kennedy's concern is to help her children understand the greatness of their father. Here, on May 29th, 1964, on the day that would have been the President's 47th birthday, she kneels with her children beside his grave at Arlington National Cemetery.

*Wide World Photos*

41. Caroline, in school uniform, walks up Fifth
Avenue with her mother. The move to New York
helped Mrs. Kennedy find the kind of privacy she
wanted for herself and the children, which she could
not get in Washington.

42. Senator Robert Kennedy with his nephew.
John's first trip to the ski slopes—perhaps he needs
a little encouragement from an expert.

43. Backstage after *The Nutcracker* at the New York City Ballet. John takes special delight in bushy eyebrows and a long nose.

44. A formal meeting between Mickey Mouse and John at the World's Fair.

45. Leaving New York for England. Mrs. Kennedy and the children
are on their way to attend the dedication of a memorial to President Kennedy
at Runnymede, and I am going with them to return to England for good.

46. The Tower of London is a great success. John likes the guns and swords, and Caroline likes the restored apartments and the Crown Jewels.

47. John crawls through the barrel of an ancient gun at the Tower of London.

48. A family profile.

49. Maud Shaw at her home in Sheerness, England. Above her desk are autographed photographs of President Kennedy and his wife, and their children, whom she took care of for seven and a half years.

reports might exaggerate the thing out of proportion, but that really Caroline had not been in danger of drowning. Mrs. Kennedy listened while I told her the story.

She nodded, "Well, it's over and done with now. If you had been there, it would never have happened at all. I don't think we should make a fuss about it."

I admired Mrs. Kennedy's attitude. She could easily have kicked up a fuss, but once an incident was over, it was closed with her. After all, Caroline was perfectly all right, and Mrs. Kennedy took the sensible view that there was no need to stir up any more trouble. The only result of that incident was that the guards kept closer to us.

I had to undergo "screening" from the Secret Service myself, about six months after we moved into the White House. I thought this a little ridiculous, since I had been there so long and had been with the Kennedys for three years. I said so to the agent, who came to me with a form requiring my antecedents right back to the year one.

"This is silly," I said. "I have been with the President and his family for years. If I were a security risk or wanted to do them harm, it would have shown up by now."

He agreed, but said orders were orders. In the end, we compromised by my giving him full details of my life since coming to the United States. However, they did take my fingerprints and checked out every detail I put down on paper. I heard later that they even checked with some of my friends in various parts of the United States to whom I wrote. I guess they picked up the addresses through the White House post office.

As I say, I missed the Secret Service men when we left the White House. They had become such good friends. One of them, Mr. Lance Landis, of Mrs. Kennedy's detail, was the one who taught me to drive. That must have been one of his more dangerous assignments!

When I first mentioned that I would like to learn to drive, he said that would be all right and that he would teach me. We were up at Hyannis Port at the time, so he got one of the cars the men used and brought it round for me. It turned out to be a Galaxie, with power steering, automatic gears and heaven knows what. Still, I got in and drove off fairly comfortably. We took a road down by the beach as it happened, and things were going along fine until Mr. Landis told me to make a turn. So I swung the wheel over. It turned so easily! Of course I turned it too far, with the result that we ended up in the sand. They had to go and get a tractor to pull the car out!

After that, I had a Ford station wagon to drive, and I managed to master that very well. That was one of the many privileges I had in the White House. If I wanted to go out, I just asked the Secret Service men, and they made arrangements for me to have the Ford for the afternoon. It was really very good of them. But as well as that, I had all the other things, too, like free medical and dental care, which came with the privilege of working in the White House.

It was all rather marvelous, especially since I was the

only alien on the whole White House staff. But then, the whole of my time with the Kennedys was something of a privilege. It is only a few people who can see a great man like John F. Kennedy close-up at work and at play with his family.

# Chapter Eleven

❀
❀  ❀

Traveling with the Kennedys could be a frantic business. Quite often, the President would suddenly decide to go to Glen Ora or Palm Beach on vacation or for a long weekend, and when he made up his mind to go, we all had to scurry round to catch up with the packing and fairly race out of the White House into the Presidential helicopter. The President had a thing about not keeping the helicopter waiting. I was told it cost a great deal to run this machine, and one of the Air Force men told me that the President was insistent on trying to keep down the costs attached to the Presidency.

A typical instance of the hurry-scurry of leaving the White House came one lunchtime. Earlier in the day, having been told that we were not, in fact, traveling to Palm Beach, I took the children to Montrose Park and stayed there playing with them and their cocker spaniel, Shannon. Since there seemed to be no hurry, we cruised back to the White House and arrived home later than usual, at about twelve-thirty. As soon as I stepped into the house, one of the ushers came running up to me. "Quick, Miss Shaw," he said. "You're leaving for Palm Beach after all, at one-thirty. Everyone has been going mad looking for you."

I hurried upstairs with the children and found Mrs. Kennedy's mother, Mrs. Auchincloss, waiting to visit with the children.

"Oh, I'm sorry," I said. "We don't really have time to talk—the President wants us away by one-thirty."

I sent the children into the bathroom to get their clothes off and wash, then went into their rooms and got a suitcase each for the three of us. I had hardly stopped to think what to take with us when one of the Secret Service men came along, looking at his watch. "Hurry, Miss Shaw," he said. "You have only forty-five minutes!"

There was no time to choose John and Caroline's clothes with any care, so one of the maids and I simply threw in a couple of armfuls of suits and dresses, complete with hangers. I scooped two lots of underwear and swimsuits for the children, pushed them into the cases and shut them. I packed for myself in about sixty seconds flat, then went into the bathroom—to find John and Caroline having a lovely splashing game together.

I clapped my hands. "Come along, children, we must *hurry*." I washed the children, told Caroline to go and put on the outfit that was laid out on her bed, scampered through to John's room and dressed him. When he was finished, I picked him up and sat him on a chair.

"Now, don't move, don't get dirty and be good while I dress myself." I always had to sit him down firmly at this stage, or he would go and roll on the floor, and within five minutes he'd be as crumpled as he was before.

I changed quickly, one eye on my watch, helped Caroline do up her buttons and shoes, combed her hair, put on her topcoat and went back to John. Of course, he had vanished! I found him lying on his stomach in the corridor, crayoning. It meant we had to wash his hands again, then put on his topcoat, brush his hair and give them both a final checkover, take them to the toilet and hand them their little attaché cases in which they kept their favorite books and toys for the journey.

Then we all took a deep breath, rang for the ushers to carry our cases down, and finally reported to Mr. Meredith that we were ready. It was twenty past one!

More often than not, we were all out of breath by the time we got into the helicopter. This took us from the White House lawn to Andrews Air Force Base, just outside Washington, and landed us next to the big Presidential jet, a magnificent airplane painted turquoise blue and white with the words "United States of America" painted along the fuselage. Inside, the plane was decorated in blue and white, with gold eagle crests on the doors and seats. It was divided into three passenger compartments. At the rear, there were seats and tables as on a normal airliner. This cabin was for the President's entourage, who always traveled with him and never seemed to stop working. Next came a smaller compartment, equipped with soft chairs and two bunks. Beyond this was a bigger lounge, where the President and Mrs. Kennedy stayed.

Flying on the Presidential airplane was always a gala day for the children, because there were little trays of candy and chewing gum laid all over the place. These were things they were normally not allowed to fill up on, but once aboard the plane they made a dive for them, and I never had the heart to stop them. We usually stayed in our compartment, where the children looked at their books or did coloring with their crayons. Sometimes, though, if the President was not too busy, I let them out to see their parents or play with some of the people on the President's staff. They adored the children and made a great fuss over them.

We usually flew down to Palm Beach for the Christmas holidays. In my early days with the Kennedys, we stayed with Mr. Joseph Kennedy in his Spanish-style house. But after John came along there was not enough room for us, and the President and Mrs. Kennedy rented a house nearby. I must admit to being a bit apprehensive of meeting Mr. Joseph Kennedy when I first went down there. I knew that he had a poor opinion of the British, an impression gained when he was U.S. Ambassador to Britain just at the outbreak of war, and wondered if he might object to his son hiring an Englishwoman as nurse to his grandchildren. But my fears were groundless; I got on very well with Ambassador Kennedy. He was kind and generous to me, and nothing like the fearsome figure many people imagined him to be. Whenever I went to his home, he greeted me with the same enthusiasm as the children and made me feel entirely welcome.

At Christmas there was always a present from him, and when I left the house, there was always a fifty-dollar bill in an envelope. I never went looking for tips of this kind, and it was extraordinarily kind of him. When he had his stroke and was partially paralyzed, I was quite upset and told Mrs. Kennedy: "It is like something happening to an old friend of mine."

"Yes," she said. "He's always been very fond of you, and he does not get too fond of everyone, I must say."

Those Christmas holidays at Palm Beach were really glorious. After all my years in the Middle East, I thought I would always enjoy the snow and the white Christmas atmosphere, but after the heavy snowfalls of Washington and the biting cold, it was absolutely marvelous to fly down to the Florida sun and spend the holiday bathing in the warm blue sea and walk on the hot beach. I was so lucky to have that sort of life.

When she was smaller, Caroline firmly believed in Santa Claus. After all, hadn't she talked to Mrs. Santa Claus?

This came about at the connivance of the President. Shortly before Christmas, Caroline was talking to her father on one of the White House telephones—Caroline was forever picking up the phone and talking to anyone who answered—and she was telling him what she was going to ask Santa Claus to bring her for Christmas.

"I wish I could telephone him and tell him," she said.

This apparently gave the President an idea, for he called up the White House switchboard and asked one of the girls to take a call from Caroline later in the day, and pretend that she was answering the phone in the Santa Claus residence. When it was all set up, the President called Caroline on the nursery extension and told her that he had managed to call Santa Claus. He asked her if she would like to speak with him.

"Oh, yes," Caroline said, her big eyes wide and shining.

The President put her through to the operator. I watched Caroline listening intently as the switch was made, then heard her talking. She looked a bit puzzled at first, for apparently Santa Claus was not at home and the voice on the other end was Mrs. Santa Claus. And when she was invited to leave a message, Caroline reeled off a whole list of presents she would like for Christmas—a list which was duly handed to the President.

Then she came scampering over to me. "Miss Shaw, Miss Shaw," she bubbled excitedly. "I've just talked to Mrs. Santa Claus!"

"Gracious me, what a lucky girl you are," I said. "Did you give a message to Santa?"

"Oh, yes, I left a whole list of presents for me and John. Do you think he will read my message?"

124

"I should think he is reading it right now," I said. It was so delightful to see Caroline then. She was absolutely beside herself with happiness.

But only last year, I had the tricky task of telling Caroline that it was not really Santa Claus who brought her presents and packages at Christmastime. I was rather sorry when one of her older cousins told her there was no such person, for it puzzled the little girl.

"Miss Shaw," she said when she came to see me with the problem, "there is a Santa Claus, isn't there? I know there is, 'cause I spoke to Mrs. Santa." It was sad to think that this little girl had to know the truth, but I softened the blow a bit by giving her, as always, a reasonable and logical explanation.

"Well now, Caroline, it's this way," I began. "It was always really Mummy and Daddy who bought you all those lovely things at Christmas, but the story of Santa Claus is a true one." Then I told her about the good St. Nicholas, who went out and gave the poor people gifts at Christmastime, and how the legend had grown and how children all over the world believed in Santa Claus.

"Then, when they grow up into big girls and boys, we tell them how it all started. Do you understand now?" Caroline nodded sagely. I think she liked the idea of being regarded as a big girl more than anything.

Then she asked, "Does John believe in Santa?"

"Yes," I said. "But he's not big enough yet to be told about him."

"Then it's a secret?" she asked.

"Yes."

"Oh goody," said Caroline. She adored having little secrets, as most little girls do.

One of our secrets was that we were blood sisters. (I am at liberty to talk about it because my little blood sister quickly went round telling her Mummy and friends!) Anyway, we went through the ceremony together of pricking our thumbs with a needle and raising a tiny speck of blood, then holding our thumbs together until our blood mingled. We were both very proud of that. Caroline has never forgotten it either, for when she came to visit my home in Sheerness and met my sister Hettie and brother Jack, she told them quite firmly that I was her blood sister forever.

Caroline—"Buttons" her father called her, because of her little button nose—was always "my bestest friend." She liked me to tell her that when she had been particularly good, just as John liked me to tell him he was "my big boy" when he had been good or specially clever. John loved to be thought a big boy, and it was one of the best ways of appealing to him, suggesting that if he did some particular thing he would be behaving like a big boy. Like all children, he responded to reason and did things even if he didn't really want to, provided you gave him an intelligent explanation of why he should do it. That is the basis of all my work with young children— always take the trouble to sort things out in their minds until they understand the whys and wherefores.

One little worry which Caroline had when John was

born was a problem that crops up every time there is a newcomer to a family, and an older child sees you spending a long time with the baby (because you have to).

"Do you love John more than me?" she asked me one day, soon after we had moved into the White House.

"No," I replied truthfully. "I have known you for three years longer than I have known John, so I couldn't love him more than you, could I? I've been your friend for three years already."

Caroline smiled. "You're still my bestest friend?"

"Of course I am and always will be," I said. She gave me a quick hug and skipped away to play, her problem solved. There was never any hint of jealousy between those two children. Caroline was so very proud of her little brother when he was a tiny baby, and even though John temporarily edged her out of the limelight, she never resented him, as can happen with older children.

But then, she is a naturally loving child, and nowhere was this more evident than in her love of animals. She inherited this from her mother, for Mrs. Kennedy has a great affection for all kinds of animals. Both mother and daughter, for instance, were wonderful horseback riders and loved to spend hours of their time in the saddle. This was in contrast to the men of the family. The President and John much preferred playing about with mechanical things, although John was devoted to his spaniel Shannon, who more or less grew up with the boy.

The family's first pet was a Welsh terrier named Charlie. He was Caroline's dog when she was much younger, and she adored him. I remember when Charlie became a father, Caroline wanted to see his offspring, so we had puppies all over the house, although we had to give them away before she got too fond of them all. Unfortunately, after leaving the White House for New York, we had to dispense with all the dogs except for the family favorite, Shannon. Charlie, in fact, did very well for himself, going to live with Mr. Foster, the Secret Service man, and his family in Washington. The President's own dog was a big Irish wolfhound who did look so much like a wolf that Caroline promptly named him "Wolfie," and that stuck to him. Mrs. Kennedy had a German police dog given to her, called Clipper, but he, too, had to go to friends when we moved to New York.

But the most hilarious pets of all were Caroline's hamsters. Those two little rascals were forever getting out of their cage and running through the second floor of the White House. Once we lost one of them for two days, and everyone from Caroline upward was practically in mourning for the poor thing, when one of the ushers found him—fast asleep in the pile carpet of the President's dressing room! Thereafter, we nearly always knew where to find him. In the end, though, those two began to breed so prolifically that we had to get rid of them. Then we had two canaries and three parakeets, which the children kept in their bedrooms, and, of course, the two ponies, Macaroni and Leprechaun, and two deer, which again had to go when we left the White House and are now in the New York Children's Zoo.

All these animals used to be kept at the White House, except the ponies, which were stabled at Middleburg. The dogs had a room just behind the Bouquet Room on the ground floor. But if the children—or Mrs. Kennedy, for that matter—could have had all the animals they liked, there would have been no room for humans in the White House.

Caroline was a natural horseback rider because she moved so well and so gracefully, with a wonderful sense of balance. She loved ballet dancing, and her grace when performing simple ballet steps was her mother's pride and joy. What impressed her father more was her ability as a swimmer. Caroline had a smooth powerful stroke in the water, but here again, she had to be almost forced to learn. The trouble was, she was just shy of letting go and trying to swim on her own. Her swimming instructor asked if I could help him get her through this difficult stage, and I took the opportunity the next time we went swimming at Hyannis Port. We waded out together in the warm blue waters of the bay, and I supported Caroline under the tummy as she practiced her swimming strokes. When she was just out of her depth, I suddenly let go of her.

"Come on, Caroline," I encouraged her. "You can swim, you know. Keep your arms and legs going, you'll do it, you see." I think she was just a little bit panic-stricken in the first few seconds, but then she found she could keep herself on top of the water and actually make progress toward the beach. I waded through the water near her, encouraging her all the time until we reached the beach again.

"Oh, Miss Shaw, I can swim," she panted. "I can swim."

"Of course you can," I said. "I always knew you could."

From that time Caroline started swimming more and more, which delighted her father, himself a strong swimmer. John was never scared of the water. So often, I would get him all dressed on the beach and turn round to help Caroline—and find him up to his waist in the water again! Then I'd just have to take him back to the house dripping wet, his little feet squelching in his shoes. But that little scamp never minded a bit. I have no doubt that he will learn to swim properly very shortly, since he always loved to throw himself into the water and scramble out, spluttering: "I can swim, Miss Shaw, can't I?"

John always wanted to keep up with his sister. He tried very hard to be as clever as Caroline when she had a craze for asking riddles. She knew hundreds of them and was forever asking me to guess them. "When is a door not a door, Miss Shaw?" she would ask. I pretended to think hard to find the answer while she clapped her hand across her mouth to suppress a giggle.

"Dear me, Caroline, I don't know," I would say.

"When the door's ajar." And with that, she would burst into fits of giggles.

Well, little John would tell me that he knew lots of riddles, too. Then, trying hard to keep his face straight, he would ask me some question. It delighted him to find that I did not know the answer—there did not usually seem to be any—and when I gave up, he'd come out with some quite irrelevant answer and chuckle hugely at his own cleverness.

The President was always fussy about the children's appearance when out in public, and he usually complimented me on the way they looked. But once I got into a spot of bother over John—because I did not know whether to follow the instructions of the President or Mrs. Kennedy! This concerned John's hair. Mrs. Kennedy wanted it to grow long, European-style. The President preferred it cut shorter, so I tried to keep the happy medium.

One Easter, when we were down at Palm Beach, the President and Mrs. Kennedy planned to take John and Caroline to church on Easter Sunday, so I was extra careful to turn the children out immaculately. The night before, I shampooed John's hair, and in the morning I combed it carefully into the fringe style that Mrs. Kennedy liked. I have a photograph, which I treasure, of the whole family together outside Mr. Joseph Kennedy's home that Sunday morning, and, in fact, this picture became a sort of family favorite in America—the demand

*131*

for it at the White House was enormous. However, there was a slight breeze that day, and John's hair, being freshly washed, began to blow about a bit. The President had a word with me about it afterward.

"Miss Shaw," he said. "Can't we cut John's hair a little?"

What could I say? I couldn't say that Mrs. Kennedy wanted it long, so I said it would be cut the next day. Well, I did trim it a bit—but not enough for the President.

He came into the nursery, took a long look at his son and turned to me.

"Miss Shaw, when are you going to cut John's hair?"

"But, sir," I said. "I have cut it, but Mrs. Kennedy . . ." I stopped before I said too much.

But the President only grinned and said, in a kind of confidential way: "I know, but let's have some of that fringe off. If anyone asks you, it was an order from the President." And he winked.

So that was how John lost his fringe! There were lots of letters to the White House when he next appeared in public with his hair cut short. Most people seemed to agree that I had done him a favor by making him look more like an American boy. I suspect that the President and Mrs. Kennedy must have had their own private joke about that, for although she looked quite aghast for a moment when she first saw John shorn, she said nothing about it to me.

Anyway, cutting John's hair at all was a major operation. I had to sit him in a chair, cover him with a sheet from the shoulders down, pop a candy in his mouth and talk to him, sing to him—anything to take his mind off the haircut. Even so, he kept on interrupting. "Have you finished, Miss Shaw?" he'd ask, trying to wriggle out of the chair.

"Soon. Just one more snip . . . and one more. . . ."

It was the same when I cut his nails; he wriggled and squirmed impatiently all the time until I at last let him go.

Caroline was quite different. Being a girl, she loved being made pretty, and let me wash and set and comb her hair without a moment's protest. She was absolutely delighted the first time I put curlers in her hair.

They both loved to dress up, of course. At the White House we had a huge trunk filled with national costumes from all over the world, many of them brought specially for the children by the heads of state who visited the White House. Yet even more fascinating than these, to Caroline, were her mother's clothes. If she could manage to get hold of one of Mrs. Kennedy's nighties and slip it on at bedtime, she counted that a great triumph, for she would not show me what she was wearing until she got into bed and slipped off her dressing gown. Then she would ask if she could keep it on.

Caroline's fascination with her mother's shoes once caused complete chaos at one of her father's press conferences. It happened shortly after the President had been elected. We were down at Palm Beach, and he held

*133*

an impromptu question-and-answer session in the court-yard of Mr. Joseph Kennedy's home. I remember watching it from an upstairs window. The session had just got into stride, when I suddenly noticed a little figure in a nightie and oversized high-heeled shoes coming through the door into the courtyard. Clack-clack-clack went the heels of her shoes as she tripped across the yard toward her father amid gales of laughter from the pressmen. I hurried down the stairs two at a time and found Caroline being led gently away from her laughing father by Mr. Pierre Salinger, the President's Press Secretary. Lots of people thought this charming intrusion was a put-up job by the President or Mr. Salinger, but I can assure you it was not.

But it did make a lovely picture of the President as a family man, to whom his children were terribly important. Throughout nearly three years at the White House, the President and Mrs. Kennedy did everything they could to remain as nearly normal a family as the pressures of the Presidency would allow.

# *Chapter Twelve*

❀

❀    ❀

Some of my most cherished memories of Caroline and John are of the days we all spent at Hyannis Port in the summer and at Palm Beach over Christmas. Both places were absolute paradise for two lively children.

For John, there was the sea and the sand. That was all he wanted in the world. He scampered and splashed, built sandcastles and demolished them with ferocious gusto—though he would get awfully mad if anyone else tampered with them. Of course there were the occasional scenes when he would come howling to me, complaining: "Caroline stepped on my castle!" And then peace could only be restored if I got down on my hands and knees and helped construct another bigger, better castle for him.

Hyannis, being the family "stronghold," was crowded with Kennedy children, and during the day everything revolved round them. In the mornings, Caroline, from the age of five, liked to go off with a group of children to go riding. John never cared much for horses, and the first time he was on a horse was not a great success. I'm afraid he did not really appreciate being so high up off the ground that day at Camp David, and not until recently did he have another shot at riding.

Mrs. Kennedy, being a fine horsewoman herself and having a daughter just as keen, naturally wanted John to take riding lessons. But after one circuit of the paddock on the back of Caroline's pony Leprechaun, his mouth turned down at the corners and he said flatly: "I wanna get off!"

John was very much more a helicopter-man than a horse-man.

So, while Caroline went off riding, John and I and our Secret Service man would go down to the beach for a swim and play until lunchtime. Lunch was very often a picnic, and the children's favorite place for eating out like this was at Egg Island, just off Hyannis. Meals that we ate on the beach there were great fun. The food was specially ordered by the children themselves, so it tended to be composed of huge quantities of ice cream, fruit and Cokes. It used to give Caroline and John a great deal of pleasure to drink unlimited supplies of Coke when we went on picnics, because they were not normally allowed to have too many sweets. I have always considered that too many candies and things like that spoil children's appetites for proper and necessary food, so I normally insisted on rationing them strictly to the odd candy and soda—and even then only after they had eaten their proper meal. However, on holiday we let that rule slide. For one thing, all the other Kennedy children were allowed to do pretty much as they pleased, and it would have been hard on Caroline and John if I had tried to keep too rigidly to nursery rules.

Anyway, they usually ate a lot of everything, and that, perhaps, was the main thing. Caroline's particular passion was hot dogs, and no matter how I tried to get her to change the menu, she always insisted on hot dogs. The more I tried to stop her, the more she would tease. Caroline adored to have little private jokes, and, if perhaps she had been out on a picnic without me, she would come running to me in the house in fits of giggles.

"Guess what I had for lunch today, Miss Shaw!"

"Mmmm. Let me see now," I would reply. "Could it possibly have been . . ."

"Hot dogs!" Caroline used to collapse with laughter at this point, and I usually had to finish by pretending to be stern with her and saying: "Well, if I'd been there you wouldn't have had hot dogs."

Caroline was such a lovely child, so full of fun like that. It absolutely delighted her to have private jokes with me, and no one else was allowed to join in.

Another regular event at Hyannis was a weekly cookout on the seashore at the West Beach club. All the children from the Kennedy families went along to them, and joined in the fun around a big bonfire on the beach. The idea was for everyone to cook his own steak, hot dogs or hamburgers, which, of course, the children just adored.

It was a wonderful sight to see them there at dusk, their faces shining with happiness in the light of the fire, holding sausages and steaks to the hot coals on long toasting forks. More often than not the things were cooked to a crisp, but it never seemed to matter, for we always ate the lot.

Before the meal, the people at the club used to arrange little swimming races between the dozens of children who gathered there. Caroline was very good at swimming, and the first time she entered she won easily. But the next time she had to give the others a head start, and she only came in third, which disappointed her terribly.

Caroline was very much a creature of moods. In something like a swimming race, for instance, she could be very good if she wanted to and was willing to fight to win. At other times, though, she simply withdrew into her shell and did not try. She was particularly susceptible to moods like that during the period after her father's death. With Caroline, it was all a question of confidence, of her being encouraged and reassured.

Not so with John, though. When he found himself in a little race with the tiny ones, he leaped into the water and splashed like fury—a complete extrovert.

Most afternoons at Hyannis Port, I used to take the children out into the country. Naturally, the Secret Service men always came with us, and they were, as usual, marvelous with the children. We never lacked something to do with those men around. We used to play ball, or the men would run races with the children or maybe just sit in the sunshine and tell stories. There were always plenty of stops on the way, too, for candy, ice cream and so on.

We had a craze for miniature golf at one time, and this Caroline thoroughly enjoyed. However, John could never get on with the game because, as he put it, "the ball never goes where I hit it, Miss Shaw." And he would get very cross and march off the green. But we had a lot of fun those afternoons.

On wet days, the children liked to go to see a film in the afternoon. This was either in the house or over at Grandpa Kennedy's home, which was equipped with a fifty-seat cinema. I used to like going to these shows myself for, apart from the Mickey Mouse and Bugs Bunny cartoons, Mr. Kennedy always had available the very latest movies, and many times I have seen films there long before they were ever released to the public.

One of the highlights of the Hyannis Port holiday was Mrs. Kennedy's birthday in June. Weeks ahead of time, the children and I would plan what they were going to give their mother as a gift. Mrs. Kennedy much preferred to have something from the children that they had made themselves, rather than anything they went into a store to buy. This seemed very sensible, and I did my best to encourage the children to make something for her, even if it was only a painting. Of course, John was too small to do anything much by himself, but nonetheless, he would get hold of a big sheet of paper and cover it with paint and "sign" his name at the bottom.

*139*

He once gave his mother a picture of me—or at least, that's what he said it was! I made a fearful blunder when he was painting it, though.

"Is that the beach you are painting, John?" I said encouragingly. And then, without waiting for a reply, I went on: "It's very good."

But with great dignity, John said: "It's not the beach. It's you."

A quick cover-up was obviously required. "Oh," I said. "I can see now. I must have been looking at it from the wrong angle."

Mrs. Kennedy was, rightly, very keen on Caroline and John using their heads and hands like this. The only pity of it was that they had so little time to spare, for they must have been the busiest children in the world. Always, they had something to do, and of course, school. It was not until bedtime that they had their quietest and most relaxed moments, when they would settle down comfortably while I read them one of their favorite stories.

They were very capable of amusing themselves, however, and both had a high degree of intelligence, as one would expect from the children of President and Mrs. Kennedy. What people did not expect, though, was that Caroline and John would be such unspoiled, nice kids. There was nothing "bratty" about them. And while I held this view myself, it was always rather rewarding when other people came to the same conclusion.

Anyway, quite apart from my own prejudice toward

them, I am convinced that Caroline and John will always be two very nice, intelligent, well-behaved children. Perhaps I was always a bit emphatic about this, for even Mrs. Kennedy would tease me about the way I praised the children behind their backs.

"Oh, Miss Shaw," she would say. "You're biased."

Well, let's face it, I am.

# Chapter Thirteen

PRESIDENT KENNEDY must have had enormous worries concerning world politics and affairs of state, the sort of worries that perhaps I could never possibly understand. But certainly I can remember that at times of stress, such as during the Cuba crisis and when the news was full of trouble with Russia, he would occasionally show signs of tiredness and strain. As far as I could tell, these signs were never terribly serious, but they were quite detectable.

Therefore, it is all the more credit to him that at no time did he ever allow his tiredness or strain to show in his everyday dealings with the children, with me or any others on the White House staff. At all times he was considerate to us all, and, no matter how pressing his duties were, he always found time to listen to the children. Of course, when he was extremely busy, he would have to curtail his visits to the children, but when he was in the

White House, he somehow always found time to see them for a little while during the day. One of his favorite things was to break off from his office work when Caroline's school was in recess at midmorning and come out on the lawn to watch them at play, for he knew I usually brought John down for a romp with the others at this time.

The President had picked up my habit of calling the children by clapping hands, and he used to come out through the glass doors of his office, stand watching the children for a while, then clap his hands a couple of times—and then he would be surrounded by children. He usually took them into his office for a minute or two and handed round the candy before shooing them out again into the sunshine.

John, especially, loved to be with his daddy. The big moments of his life came when he was allowed to travel with the President in the helicopter, and on those occasions when he could not go, it was always difficult to explain to the little chap that he had to stay behind this time. But some of the finest times the President had with his son were at Camp David, a Presidential retreat in the mountains, which was the nearest the President could go to get "away from it all" while only half an hour from Washington. We used to go down there in the summer for long weekends. John was always torn between going by helicopter or car. But when we could not use the chopper, we used to make up for the disappointment by stopping in at the snake farm at the foot of the mountains, where the children, bless them, used to play with the snakes! There was a big tame cobra called George who was a great favorite with Caroline and John, and their game was to let the snake slide up their arms and then offer him to me.

"Here, Miss Shaw," they used to say. "You take George." They knew very well that I would recoil in fright. I could never stand the beastly things, but they held no terrors for the children.

If the children and I went on ahead of the President and Mrs. Kennedy, John would always keep an ear out for the arrival of the helicopter with his father on board. Often we went down there on a Friday afternoon, and the President joined us on Saturday morning. That meant John hovering all the time around the landing patch, looking up in the sky for the first sight of the whirlybird or the first sound of its clattering blades. When he heard it, he used to dance with delight.

"The chopper's coming, Miss Shaw," he would pipe. "The chopper's coming."

As soon as it landed and the motor stopped, John used to bound across to greet his father, and they had a little talk together on the tarmac. But very often on those relaxed weekends, John dragged his father—who came not too unwillingly, either—round to the helicopter hangar, and there they played games. John liked to put on the pilot's helmet and push the control stick around and press the buttons, flicking the switches and making all the right noises for starting up and taking off. I have one wonderful memory of the time when I went looking for John on a Saturday afternoon. For the most part, I left Caroline to her own devices—she was usually riding— since she was the older of the two, and kept my eye on John. This time, I had a good idea where he would be— down in the hangar. Sure enough, he was. And so was the President. Both of them were sitting at the controls of the helicopter with flying helmets on. The President was playing the game seriously with his son, taking orders from Flight Captain John, thoroughly absorbed in the whole thing. I retreated quietly and left father and son very happy together.

Looking back now, I think that one of the things poor John missed most when we left the White House was the trips he made with his father in the chopper.

But the President's fondness for playing with his children whenever he could rebounded on us all on one hilarious occasion. This time he had been playing a game in his office with Caroline. She had taken down with her one of her dolls, a big walking, talking dolly that contained a miniature tape machine, so designed that when you spoke to it and then pressed the button at the back, the doll repeated what you had said to it. It was a fascinating thing for Caroline to play with, and she spent hours "teaching the dolly to talk." However, this time she must have left it down in her father's office, for when it was brought back to the nursery the following day, I happened to press the button to hear what Caroline had been teaching the doll—and I heard the unmistakable Boston tones of the President himself.

What's more, he was giving vent to his feelings about something or other and used a very naughty word! It was very unlike him to use language like that, for I had never heard him swear before. But there was no mistaking this particular epithet!

I knew jolly well that something had to be done before Caroline came back from school, for if she heard the word in her father's voice, she was very likely to start using it herself. So I tried to erase the President's words by saying something to the doll myself.

However, there did not seem to be any way of winding the tape back, so all I got was the sound of my voice, preceded by the President's—and still we had that word. In desperation, I asked one of the Secret Service men to come and help me, but he was unable to get the tape to wind back either. In the end, we had to take the back off the doll altogether and take the complete tape out and throw it away. Caroline was a little puzzled about it all when she came home from school, but I told her that the doll had temporarily lost her voice. And she did not get her voice back until one of the Secret Service men had been to a store and bought another tape to fit into her!

The peril of children picking up undesirable language is something that every parent knows, and it is bound to happen when somebody says something in an unguarded moment. You can bet your bottom dollar that when some-

*147*

body does say something, the children's ears pick it up as accurately as a radar set. Caroline, at one stage, heard someone using the word "damn." Sure enough, I caught her saying it once when something went wrong. Of course, it is disastrous to make a thing out of it, so I said nothing until later in the day, when I happened to drop the soap out of my hand into the bath when I was washing Caroline.

"Jam," I said. Immediately, Caroline's ears pricked up.

"What did you say, Miss Shaw?" she asked.

"Jam," I said. "I always say that when I drop things."

"Why?" she asked.

"I don't know really," I said. "Come to think of it, it is a bit silly of me, isn't it?" Caroline giggled.

"Oh well," I said, "if you think it's silly of me, I don't think I'll say it any more." She went on playing with the ducks in the water and said no more. But I didn't hear her use the word "damn" any more. A little bit of subterfuge is a useful thing with little ones!

Caroline and John knew exactly how to behave on formal occasions. As soon as they were old enough, Caroline was taught to curtsy and John to bow, and we had some fine old giggles when we rehearsed them together. Caroline became very adept at her curtsies, but she nearly toppled right over when she produced one superlative effort at a reception for King Saud of Arabia. She went down so far on one knee that she very nearly lost her balance and fell right over. However, she recovered with all her natural grace, to the delight of the King. This tall, bearded man was captivated by the delightful little girl and gave her a kiss, which sent Caroline running out of the Oval Room, red-faced with blushes.

"He's a nice man," she whispered, "but I wish he wouldn't kiss me. It tickles!"

Another royal visitor to the White House was the Shah of Iran and his beautiful wife, Queen Farah Diba, herself a young mother. She became particularly fond of John, who was at that time only about a year old, and she and Mrs. Kennedy spent quite a long time together discussing their children.

Of course, if either of the children were going to do anything wrong, it had to be John, yet I can only recall the little scamp letting us down once—and even then it was not entirely his fault. This happened at the reception for the heads of the Grand Duchy of Luxembourg. I had dressed both the children carefully and rehearsed them, as usual, with their bows and curtsies. Then I brought them down to the reception and waited outside. But this time I was called in to take John out and deal with him, for instead of being introduced properly, he just threw himself on the floor and would not bow.

When I got him outside, I scolded him: "What on earth did you do that for?" I asked. "That's not being my big boy, is it?"

John looked up at me tearfully. "But Miss Shaw, they didn't give me my cookie." John was usually given a cookie and a drink of ginger ale at these receptions, but this time there were so many people there that they forgot to give John anything, and he got upset about it. I felt a certain sympathy for him, but I had to give him a bit of a lecture about never again making such a spectacle of himself—and, to his credit, he never did.

It was a great experience for me to live in the White House with America's First Family. There was always something going on, someone important arriving or visiting, and I felt privileged to be the only foreigner, so to speak, to live there amid such important happenings. It was the absolute pinnacle of my career, and a unique position for an Englishwoman.

When there were big White House functions, Caroline and I occasionally crept down the front stairs and sat together watching the goings-on through the banisters. It was terribly exciting for a little girl to see all the people dressed in their evening dresses, glittering with jewelry, and waiting in line to be introduced to the President. Once, the line of people broke up in confusion because some of them spotted Caroline and came over to see her. They made such a fuss over her that the President came over and took us down to meet his guests.

Caroline used to love those moments, for she was a great favorite with the musicians who played in the White House band. I remember the first important reception that President and Mrs. Kennedy held there. Caroline and I came down to have a look at the people coming into the house, and she began waving to the red-coated musicians. After a little while, the band suddenly struck up a nursery rhyme tune in her honor, and she clapped her hands delightedly. Mrs. Kennedy heard it, and looked over to the staircase and spotted us.

"Bring Caroline down," she called, and so we made an entrance among a whole gathering of important people while the band played some more children's favorites. Caroline went over to the band after a while and spoke to the conductor, who asked her if she had liked the little selection he played.

"Yes," she said. "Can you please play some more?"

In the end, they devoted half the evening to nursery tunes, much to the delight of Caroline and, I'm sure, of everyone else.

On one of those great occasions, I was introduced to the British Prime Minister, Mr. Harold Macmillan—by the President himself. This happened just after I had tucked the children down for the night. I was walking along the corridor and met the President.

"Can you come in here a moment, Miss Shaw?" he called.

I patted my hair and smoothed my dress and walked across the corridor into the Oval Room, where the reception for the Prime Minister was being held. The President took me by the arm and led me across to Mr. Macmillan.

"I thought you might like to meet someone from your own country," the President said to Mr. Macmillan.

The Prime Minister stood up and shook hands with me when the President introduced us. He said it was nice to

*151*

know that the President's children were in such good hands. We chatted inconsequently for a few minutes, and I wished the Prime Minister a pleasant visit and left.

By this time I must have been properly Americanized, for I thought the interview a little starchy, and could not help comparing the stiff and formal manner of the Prime Minister with the easygoing and relaxed approach of the American leaders I had met, such as the late Mr. Adlai Stevenson and other close friends of the Kennedys. I was very sad when Mr. Stevenson died in London recently. He was always such a charming person, and, when he came to the White House, he very often stopped for a chat with me. I liked him tremendously, and the children warmed to him from the first.

Mrs. Kennedy was particularly keen on allowing the children to meet the people who came to the White House. It was part of her effort to make them feel all part of a family and just like other children. There were times—like the Ben Bella incident, for instance—when I had to take the children away, but as far as it was possible, the President and Mrs. Kennedy always liked their children to be near them, as much like a normal family as possible. For my part, I always tried to keep to this principle. Which is why I always changed into "mufti" whenever I went out with the children. In my white nurse's uniform, the Kennedy children were too easily recognized, as I found out one time after taking Caroline for a look at the shops in Washington. She loved window-gazing and nosing around the shops, and I, of course, loved to stroll along window-shopping. This time, we went into a five-and-ten-cent store.

We were standing near one of the counters, and Caroline was trying to see up to the imitation jewelry, which had caught her eye. She was only three at the time, and still rather shy at meeting strangers, so I held on to her hand and tried to keep her incognito. I had just bent down to say something to her, and I straightened up to see a woman bearing down on us with a pen and paper thrust toward Caroline.

"Oh, it's Caroline Kennedy, isn't it?" the woman boomed. "Do give me your autograph, dear." Little Caroline retreated behind the skirt of my white dress in the face of this onslaught, and the whole episode made me furious.

"How silly can you be?" I said sharply to the woman. "The child can't even write yet. For heaven's sakes, go away."

I must say the woman blushed and backed away hurriedly, but I took Caroline's hand and led her out of the store before anyone else gathered round us. I am quite sure that had Mrs. Kennedy been there with us, she would have dealt with the whole thing a lot more graciously than I—she is an expert at handling all types of people in all sorts of situations—but I was very cross that someone could be so stupid as to embarrass and upset Caroline. Anyway, that was the last time I ever went out in public with my uniform on.

Inside the White House, the children had a wonderful

time whenever there was a big musical or artistic occasion. There was a ballet performance staged one time at the invitation of Mrs. Kennedy—a devotee of the fine arts—when all the artists moved into the White House for the day to prepare for the occasion and to rehearse. I took Caroline down to their temporary dressing rooms, and we watched them make up and put on their wigs and costumes. She really was enthralled at it all, for she had her mother's love of dancing and music. And, I must say, I learned a lot in those couple of hours, too.

Another instructive hour for me was the time that Mrs. Kennedy did her TV tour of the White House, playing hostess to millions of viewers, showing them the art treasures of the President's home and tracing the history of the house, the pictures, pottery, furniture and objects of interest. It is a strange thing, but living inside the White House, I was so close to all these things that I had missed a lot of their significance.

But Mrs. Kennedy opened my eyes—as well as those of people of many nations—to these beautiful things. Her performance was quite masterly for the way in which she was so composed, knowledgeable and entirely interesting. The whole program was her own idea, for she always felt strongly that the White House belonged to the people of the United States. All the decorations and additions that she had put in when her husband became President were intended not so much for her own gratification but as a way of putting the mark of the Kennedy era on the perpetual home of American Presidents.

Yes, Mrs. Kennedy is a remarkable woman. I say that sincerely, knowing better than most people the depth of character and strength that lies within her. For I saw tragedy strike her cruelly, twice within six months, and through this came to admire her more than ever.

# *Chapter Fourteen*

❁

❁    ❁

On JULY 1, 1963, I went with Mrs. Kennedy and the children to Hyannis Port where, for the summer holidays, the President had rented a house on Squaw Island, right on the tip of a peninsula overlooking the beach and the sea. As always, the summer holiday was an exciting event, but this time there was extra excitement, for Mrs. Kennedy was expecting a third child. The baby was due in October, and for weeks before the holiday, it had been the big event in the children's lives. The whole family had agreed that if it were a boy, the baby would be called Patrick, after the President's father, whose second name was Patrick. Caroline had her own ideas of a name, should the baby be a girl. She wanted the name Susan.

We had been at Squaw Island for five weeks—it was August 7—and I was about to go for my weekly day off, when I noticed that Mrs. Kennedy was looking rather pale and worn-out.

"I won't take the day off today," I told her. "You're not looking too well. I'll stay with the children."

Well, Mrs. Kennedy was never the one to harp on illness or anything like that. "Oh no you don't," she said. "You go off and enjoy your free day. I'll look after the children."

Anyway, rather against my judgment, she persuaded me she could manage all right, and I went off to meet a friend for the day. We went swimming at Sandwich, a few miles from Hyannis Port, and when we got in the car to head back, I switched on the radio and heard a newscast: Mrs. Jacqueline Kennedy had been rushed to the specially prepared maternity unit at Otis Air Force Base nearby, since her baby was expected prematurely.

I hurried back to Squaw Island to take charge of Caroline and John. Later in the day their baby brother was born—Patrick—but all was not well. The baby was rushed to a Boston hospital and put in the latest type of incubator. The President stayed in Boston for the next two days, watching over his son until all hope had gone, and poor Patrick died. It was a sad time for all of us.

In due course, John was told that he would not have a baby brother after all. Of course, he was too young to understand. But the news brought tears to Caroline's eyes, though she did not cry. That night the three of us knelt and said a special prayer for Patrick and for Mummy and Daddy.

Mrs. Kennedy came home after eleven days in the hospital and spent a couple more weeks in bed, away from everyone but the children. She had a room with a big sun lounge where she could look out over the beach and the sea. The weather that year was very good, and for the children and myself, life went on much as usual. We went swimming, played on the sand, had cookouts and went for walks. But I did try to keep them a little quieter near the house. Actually, Mrs. Kennedy made a much better recovery than I expected. By the time we returned to Washington, in mid-September, she appeared to be all right.

Gradually, Mrs. Kennedy regained her normal vitality and became once more involved in the whirl of her life and duties as America's First Lady, proving once more that work is the best therapy of all.

The Kennedys became a happy, tight-knit family again. Caroline went back to school, the President worked as hard as ever and Mrs. Kennedy began to recover. She was due to make her first public appearance in Dallas, Texas.

None of us could possibly guess that more tragedy, more terrible agony, was soon to hit this fine family.

The President's trip to Dallas was to be one of those periodic speechmaking tours that any President with his eye on the next election has to make. It was to be a show-the-flag visit to the South to consolidate the personal popularity of the Kennedys. Mrs. Kennedy went along on the tour. She was always tremendously popular wherever she went, and together she and the President always made a handsome couple, the very epitome of the young

*159*

family people that Americans adore—especially if, like the Kennedys, they combine charm with ability enough to achieve the very heights of success.

It was an odd thing, I think, that the Americans only went wholeheartedly for President Kennedy once he had scraped into the White House. He was by no means an overwhelming choice in the 1960 Presidential election, for he won it by a matter of thousands of votes from an electorate of millions. And yet, once in the White House his popularity grew and grew, as he proved himself an able leader and a fine man. To me, it was the greatest tragedy of this century that he had to be cut down by a madman on the very threshold of real greatness, which I am sure he would have achieved had he been allowed to live.

I last saw President Kennedy in the elevator on the second floor of the White House, minutes before he left on that final, fatal trip to Dallas. There were no special good-byes that time. The President and Mrs. Kennedy were to be away only a few days and planned to be back in time for John's birthday on November 25th, and Caroline's two days after that.

On the morning of the 21st, when they left for the South, they decided to slip away as quietly as they could from the children. Caroline was due in school anyway, and after saying good-bye to her parents, she went up to the White House roof to wave to the helicopter as it took off from the lawn. John went with his parents to the helicopter, but I left them at the lift.

They stepped in, and the three of them waved to me.

"Good-bye. Safe journey home." Those were the last words I spoke to the President.

The odd thing about that day was that John did not cry when he left his parents. I think it was the first time ever that he did not cry to go aboard the aircraft with his father. Usually we had a hard time convincing him that he was not going. This time, however, he was as good as gold and just waved happily and then came back to me in the White House, quite content. In retrospect, it struck me as strange, though at the time, I think I just ticked it off in my mind as another corner turned in John's growing-up process.

The White House functioned smoothly as always. No one could have forecast the shattering news that was to throw everything into chaos and bring tragedy and grief into the lives of so many people. That, as I have said, struck us all at lunchtime the next day.

# *Chapter Fifteen*

THE FOUR OF US sat silently in the back of the big black car as it turned onto Pennsylvania Avenue. I deliberately did not look back at the White House now that we had left it for good, and in such unhappy circumstances. It felt like leaving home, knowing I would never go back. My gloom was shared, of course, by Mrs. Kennedy and the children. Even John was quiet throughout the journey to N Street, where we were about to move into our temporary home before leaving for Palm Beach. Christmas was only three weeks away, but I never felt less festive in my life. All the shops in Washington had switched on colored lights, and there were holly wreaths on the doors of houses, but now all the merriment had gone out of Christmas, overshadowed as it was by the tragedy of President Kennedy's death.

Mr. Harriman's house on N Street was a very lovely place. They had left some of the servants there to help us move in and take care of Mrs. Kennedy. Two White House maids had also come over to help us all unpack. I went with Caroline and John straight up to our rooms on the third floor. There was no elevator in the house, and I remember John being quite put out at having to walk up-stairs.

In our rooms, we unpacked our suitcases. Caroline had brought her favorite toys with her—a doll's pram, her best dressing-up doll called Mary, her ever-faithful Raggedy-Ann and the toy poodle Tinkerbelle. John had brought his usual armory of guns and swords and a few mechanical toys. He had been given a Marine uniform for his birthday a few days before, and I remember we had to bring that with us; he wore it almost constantly. I went to bed that night, wondering what Christmas would be like this year at Palm Beach. Mrs. Kennedy had rented the usual house on the beach, near the President's fa-ther's home. Princess Radziwill and her husband and two children were to stay with us as they always did. I deter-mined that, as far as possible, I would help make it a happy time for the children, knowing full well that noth-ing could make it as joyous as other Christmases. I thought back to other years, when Christmas always ar-rived in a kind of happy panic for the Kennedys.

Last time, I remembered, the President had gotten be-hind in sending out his and Mrs. Kennedy's personal cards, and he roped me in to help. He called out as I was going past the sitting-room door.

"Hey, Miss Shaw," he called. "Come and help us lick a few stamps."

Mrs. Kennedy had shaken her head in despair at her husband. "Miss Shaw doesn't want to lick our stamps, Jack. I'll bet she has got enough of her own."

The President grinned. "Aw, you don't mind, do you Miss Shaw? Here, get a hold of this lot." And he passed me a great bundle of envelopes and stamps, and we spent an hour all licking and sticking stamps until the chore was done. Such happy memories. . . .

Caroline was still attending school at the White House each day until it broke up for the Christmas holidays, but I did not take her over myself, leaving it to the Secret Service detail, who still shadowed the children everywhere. Mrs. Kennedy spent a lot of time going to the Arlington cemetery to visit the President's grave, and praying quietly and alone at the cathedral in Washington. John and I carried on our lives more or less normally. He played and scampered and chatted as much as ever, but I could not help noticing his bright little face clouding over sometimes as he struggled to understand what had happened to him. He often asked why we were not still living in the "other house" and similar questions, and it was with some relief that we eventually traveled down to Palm Beach and away from Washington.

Mrs. Kennedy did very well that Christmas in making it a good time for the children. She was a sad figure, and I felt a tremendous sympathy for her and admired her a great deal for the effort she made for John and Caroline. The house was so full of memories for us all, though, that when the children went to bed in the evening it was difficult to prevent that sadness from spreading through the house again.

Caroline and I dressed the Christmas tree together, putting up the lights and the glittering stars and baubles, while John added his little bits to the lower branches and threw tinsel over everything and everyone. Mrs. Kennedy hung up the stockings over the fireplace with all our little presents in them, leaving the other gaily wrapped parcels all around the tree. We all got up and had breakfast on Christmas morning before opening our presents, but as soon as the meal was finished, the living room became steadily more and more strewn with wrapping paper, boxes, ribbons and heaps of new dolls, airplanes, cars, games, dressing-up suits, toy animals and candy. There were hugs and kisses and thank yous and a great deal of shouting and laughter, which became so infectious that the grown-ups temporarily forgot the grief of a month before and joined in.

In the afternoon, Caroline, John and their two cousins put on their usual Nativity play for us, proudly acting out the Christmas story in front of us all. It was sad and touching, and seeing the children there strengthened my resolve to help Mrs. Kennedy and her children in any way I could to regain their balance.

There were still questions, of course, from Caroline— some of them so simple yet so poignant. It made me marvel at the uncomplicated workings of a child's mind. Once, just before dinner, she asked me if God would give her father something to do in Heaven.

I said I expected so.

"What do you think he is doing, then?"

"Well . . ." I thought for a moment. "I should think God has made him guardian angel over you and John and Mummy, so that he can still watch over you all."

Caroline asked if Patrick could help their father.

"Yes, he will," I said. "They'll keep each other company."

I did not know whether I was doing right or wrong in answering her questions like that, but I always thought it right to give the children something to believe in, something to hang on to, so that they would believe at least that their father was happy and still an influence on them. Later, I told Mrs. Kennedy about these conversations.

She was relieved to know that Caroline had accepted the fact of her father's death and had been set at ease about things which seemed unimportant to us, perhaps, but which were of vital importance to her. I discussed with Mrs. Kennedy how I should answer the children's questions about their father, and she was firmly of the opinion that, having had such a wonderful man for a father, they should grow up knowing all about him. I never spun them fairy tales about him, but always tried to answer their questions in a way that was both encouraging and correct. It was Mrs. Kennedy's aim to make her children proud of their father, so that they were always

167

aware of what he was and who he was. And I think she has succeeded well in substituting pride in his achievements and his memory for lingering sorrow at his death.

We returned to Washington in January, 1964, by which time Mrs. Kennedy had completed negotiations to buy a house of her own—just across N Street, at number 3017.

This house had been standing empty for some time and had to be completely redecorated, so it provided an opportunity for Mrs. Kennedy to busy herself with color schemes, furniture arrangement, wallpapers and all the other intricacies of decor which fascinated her. I was very glad to see her busy again, running back and forth across the street a dozen times a day to supervise the work. Once again, she was determined to make the move as quickly as possible. She had the decorators working two shifts a day, through Saturdays and Sundays, so as not to waste a moment.

It was a pity that the children and I did not have very much chance to help during this preparatory stage, for we had problems of our own. As soon as we arrived back from Palm Beach, Caroline fell sick with chicken pox, and sure enough, within a couple of days, John came down with it as well. I think this was the first time either of them had been actually ill enough to be confined to bed, and they reacted to the prospect of four days' confinement in their individual ways. Caroline was a good patient. She read books, did puzzles, made colored pictures and kept herself well wrapped up in her bed. But

John was quite impossible. Nothing I said, no amount of lecturing would keep him between the sheets. Every time I went out of the room, he'd throw back the covers and hop out of bed. It was so funny, because I used to go out of the room and wait outside his door, knowing full well what he was going to do. I would hear his little feet padding across the bedroom carpet, the door would open ever so slowly and then his head popped round the doorpost, his face bright with mischief.

"John!" I'd say reproachfully.

"All right, Miss Shaw," he'd say with all the weary frustrations of a little boy who simply could not understand why the grown-ups wanted to keep him trapped in his bed. "I'm going back."

Then I'd tuck him in again while he sat up against the pillows making big sighing sounds. But I knew it was all a waste of time. The moment I left the room, he'd be out again, hunting for his toys or looking out of the window. The only consolation was the thought that if he was lively enough to keep getting up, he wasn't too ill.

The first day the children were allowed out of the house after their illness was the day we moved across to No. 3017, early in February. Even such a short-distance move meant a great deal of work for everyone. Obviously, we could not just have the furniture and so on carried across the street, so a couple of big trucks loaded up with the stuff, circled round the block and came back across the other side of the street and unloaded it!

No. 3017 was a lovely three-story house, not quite typical of the narrow-fronted houses of Georgetown, for here the rooms were larger than one normally found. Mrs. Kennedy had done the place up beautifully and with exquisite taste. She was waiting for the three of us when we hurried across the street to our new home. For the first time in weeks, she looked really flushed with happiness. She was in the hallway, dressed in a kind of smock and wearing flat-heeled shoes, directing the moving men when we came up the steps.

"Welcome home," she said.

I stopped and looked around me. "Oh, this is a lovely house, Mrs. Kennedy," I said. "It feels like home. I am sure you and the children are going to be happy here."

"Yes," she said. "I hope so, anyway."

It has always struck me as a terrible pity that it did not work out that way for her. It didn't, because people would not let her settle down and forget. There was never a time when there were not crowds of sightseers gathered outside, waiting to see her and the children, taking photographs and trying to peep into the windows. The public had such sympathy for Mrs. Kennedy—it was such a pity that their curiosity spoiled her chances of happiness in this lovely old house.

However, when we first moved in, everyone was delighted. John was very relieved to find an elevator to take a load off his little legs.

"Miss Shaw," he piped. "There's an elevator. Come on, let's try it out." So we had to squash into the thing and ride up to our rooms on the third floor. The elevator was built, I should think, to take no more than one adult and a small suitcase, but we crushed in there somehow—me, John, Caroline and the spaniel Shannon—and the poor old lift groaned under the weight of us. But I must say it stood up to us well, for every time we came in, we all squeezed ourselves in while John shut the gates and pushed the button for us.

The children and I lived up on the top floor in a more or less self-contained suite, with a room each, bathrooms and a big playroom for Caroline and John. This was the first time they had been allotted a playroom, which was something I had always thought a good idea. The room had originally been assigned to me, but when Mrs. Kennedy first showed me around the house, I protested that the room was really far too large for me and suggested making it into a playroom for the children. But, big as it was, the room was quickly filled with toys which the children had not seen for nearly three months, having been in storage since we left the White House.

When all the packing cases arrived from the warehouse, the children had a gala day. I had everything moved into the playroom, and together we began unpacking about forty boxes and trunks. There were great squeals of delight from them both when they rediscovered old treasures—long-forgotten dolls, playsuits, old hats, clockwork motor cars, books, cuddly toys and a hundred and one exciting things. John found an old machine gun and went round the room firing the thing off. Caroline became absorbed in dressing up an old favorite doll; a construction kit fell out of its box and scattered all over the floor; John played "armies" with a model fort; Caroline went for a walk across the room with a battery-driven dog, and somewhere under all the debris an electric-train set lay half-assembled. The pandemonium and the mess was indescribable, but I have rarely seen the children as excited and pleased with themselves. It even had the edge on Christmas, I think, for they seized their old toys affectionately, like old friends.

The room was soon crammed with their things. In the corner stood Caroline's doll house and a big rocking pony. She loved that thing. It was almost as big as she was, and was covered in real horseskin and had a real saddle. It was her pride and joy. John, who wasn't at all "horsy," did not play with that, but had his own nearly life-size tiger on wheels, which had pride of place on his side of the room. At the time of the President's death, the children received more toys than ever from well-wishing people all over the world. Of course, they could not possibly keep them all, but I do remember that John got a huge tile construction kit and Caroline a sewing machine.

I forget who sent them, but I do know that these two items kept the children amused for hours on end, for, in their different ways, these things fitted their personalities perfectly. Caroline had great patience and would carefully stitch dolls' dresses which I cut out for her, and John loved to sit on the floor with his kit, rapidly fitting together the tiles to make houses and garages and forts.

The playroom window overlooked N Street, and it was

from there that we always watched when Mrs. Kennedy went out or anyone important came to the house. But the children's favorite lookout place was a kind of skylight dome on the roof. They had this kind of construction on the roofs of many houses in Hyannis Port and other similar fishing villages; it provided a lookout shelter for the occupants to see when the fishing boats were coming in from sea. Ours in Washington, though, provided John with many hours of amusement. I used to go up with him while he played at being a submarine captain or a soldier sentry, and I liked being up there myself, looking out over the lovely city of Washington.

The children's rooms were decorated in similar style to those in the White House—blue for John and pink for Caroline. Mrs. Kennedy had always said that Caroline could choose her own wallpaper later on, but unfortunately, we were not in the house long enough for her to do so. I had one of the guest rooms at the back, overlooking the paved garden with its old tree in the middle where the children loved to play. John had learned to ride a bike by this time and spent hours whizzing around out there in "the yard."

As I say, we were all happy there in N Street at first. We had come full circle in a way, having first lived on N Street, then moved to the White House, and now we were back on N Street again. Somehow it seemed fitting that we should come back here. Being part of a family which had now become even more close-knit by tragedy, I myself felt closer to Mrs. Kennedy than ever before. I ad-

*173*

mired her tremendously at this time, for the way in which she tried so hard to keep up a brave face, although she still mourned her husband.

Thousands of letters of condolence were still pouring in every week from all over the world, and she struggled to reply to them all. Flowers for her came almost daily. The same Secret Service men were still assigned to Mrs. Kennedy and the children; they had an office in the basement where they checked and sorted all the parcels and things addressed to Mrs. Kennedy. I was glad that the children still had the same trio of agents to care for them. They really loved the children, and John and Caroline regarded them with tremendous affection.

One poignant memory I have of those men was of the day when we rode in the procession from the White House to the Capitol for the President's funeral service. John and Caroline and I rode in a car going at walking pace and followed by a long file of heads of state from all over the world. On each side of the car there was a Secret Service man, also walking. And from the moment we moved off, Caroline reached out of the window on her side and clung on to the hand of Bob Foster and held it tight all the way to the Capitol. Foster told me later he had a very hard job not to weep, so touched was he by this gesture of trust by the little girl.

But I have so many happy memories of the days we spent with these fine men. Mr. Meredith usually came with us when we went for a drive in the country, and he would stop and buy doughnuts for the children and sing to them as we went along. He had a fine voice and played the piano well, too, and had a seemingly endless repertoire of songs to keep the children amused. Bob Foster was a great storyteller. Having children of his own, he knew just how to tell children a story, and in the end, John and Caroline would demand a fresh story every time we went out together. I must admit he never failed to think of one. The men were all very sad that they had to leave us when we moved to New York. They all said they would have volunteered to move with us had the job been a permanent one, but since Mrs. Kennedy and the children would have Secret Service protection for only two years, they could not afford to sell up and move from Washington and then perhaps have to move back again afterward.

I am sure Mrs. Kennedy was reluctant to leave Washington where she had so many friends, where her mother and relatives lived, but it was obvious that the continual stares of the people who gathered day after day outside No. 3017 upset her.

"I do wish they would go away," she said one day. "I know they mean well, but I can't stand being stared at like that every time I go out on the street."

It got on the children's nerves, too, I'm afraid. "What are these silly people taking my picture for?" John used to ask, when sightseers flashed off cameras at us going in and out of the house.

In a way, I suppose you could not blame people for wanting to see Mrs. Kennedy and the children, but they made a nuisance of themselves. They used to try and peep into the dining-room window on the ground floor, and although there were net curtains across it, Mrs. Kennedy used to complain that she felt overlooked every time she sat down for a meal.

Even so, I was surprised at the suddenness of our leaving Washington. I had been back on a short holiday to England, and on my return to Washington, I rang Mrs. Kennedy, who had gone to Hyannis Port with the children, to ask her when I should join them in Massachusetts.

"Come up right away if you can," she said. "And pack up your things. We are not going back to Washington. I've taken an apartment in New York."

It was just like that. After more than six years in the capital, we never again went back to live in Washington.

# Chapter Sixteen

❋

❋ ❋

Hʏᴀɴɴɪꜱ ᴘᴏʀᴛ saw the usual glorious gathering of the Kennedy clan, the whole family of brothers and sisters and their many children taking over the "compound" for their summer vacation. These were in many ways sad days for Mrs. Kennedy. So many of the old memories must have flooded back. Still, I feel she wanted to be with her relatives more than ever for the sake of the children. All the Kennedys made a little extra fuss over John and Caroline without it being too obvious, and Mr. Robert Kennedy particularly devoted himself to them. I very much admire the way he has filled the gap left by the death of his brother in the lives of Caroline and John, and there is no doubt that it is he upon whom they now look as the father figure in their lives. You have only to see them with him to realize that.

One tiny incident that really brought this home happened earlier this year when Caroline and I had just left the apartment in New York and met Robert Kennedy walking along Fifth Avenue. "There's Bob," cried Caroline, and she ran to him and jumped up into his arms. It was exactly the way she had always run to her father, jumping up in full confidence that he would catch her. It was very touching to see how kind he was to both children, and I am sure he will always do everything he can to fill the void in both their lives.

By that time in Hyannis Port, in July of 1964, Caroline was beginning to get over the shock of the President's death and was able to talk about him without too much emotion. I remember, for example, one occasion when she was reluctant to join some other children for a sail in the bay.

I said, "Daddy would be very pleased if you had a try at it. You know how proud of you he was when you started swimming, because he was a good swimmer himself. Now, he was very good at sailing. He'd be proud if you did well at that too."

I'm glad to say that she thoroughly enjoyed herself, and turned out to be very adept at sailing.

What was hard for John to accept was that he no longer lived in the "big white house" in Washington. Whenever he saw a photograph of it, he would frown and ask me: "That's where we live, isn't it, Miss Shaw?"

"No, John, we don't live there any more, do we? Don't you remember we moved into another house with Caroline and Mummy?"

He'd nod and say he remembered it, but it was some

178

time before I heard him telling Caroline, when they were both looking at a picture of the White House, "That's where we *used* to live, Caroline."

We moved to New York in September into an apartment in the Carlyle Hotel on Madison and 76th. We only stayed there for six weeks, while the decorators were busy preparing our new, permanent home at 1040 Fifth Avenue, where Mrs. Kennedy still lives now. It was very enjoyable to be back in New York, for there was so much for all of us to do there. I had a great many friends in the city, and through them, Caroline and John met a larger circle of friends. But the big event of the Kennedy family at that time was Caroline going to her first real school.

She went to the school at the Convent of the Sacred Heart on Fifth Avenue at 90th Street late in September, but the excitement of it all began weeks before while we were staying with Mrs. Auchincloss at Newport, Rhode Island. This was where Caroline first tried on her school uniform, which consists of a gray jumper, white blouse, gray jacket, with a red beret and a camel topcoat. She looked absolutely charming in the outfit, and was immensely proud of herself. She was very impatient when I had to make small alterations in the skirt, and she could hardly bear to put it all away and wait for school to begin.

That morning at the Carlyle Hotel, Caroline was up at the crack of dawn to put on her uniform—which meant that we all got up early to see her off in plenty of time. Mrs. Kennedy took Caroline herself that first day, but

Caroline insisted that John and I go down and wave her off.

Caroline has always been extremely happy at that school, though she could not quite understand all the fuss that was made over her at the beginning.

"I expect it is because you are such a nice little girl, Caroline," I said. I knew that she was bound to be the center of curiosity for a little while, but this subsided before long and she is now treated the same as any of the other children.

Caroline is a very good and bright scholar. When she brought home her first school report at Christmas last year, there was terrific excitement in the apartment when we saw how well she had done. She got an A-plus in English and writing, and was exceptionally good in French, which delighted Mrs. Kennedy, who, of course, speaks that language fluently. I was extremely proud of Caroline, especially since I had a hand in getting her started in writing and reading when she was tiny. She was always quick on the uptake in all sorts of ways, and it was not surprising that she took to school readily. In fact she gained such confidence in herself that I was able to challenge her to do even better—and she did.

One afternoon she came home with a gold medal awarded to her at school for deportment.

"Look, Miss Shaw," she said. "I have a medal."

"Oh, Caroline, we are all so proud of you. What did you get it for?" I asked.

"Deportment," she replied.

"Deportment? Oh well, of course you got a medal for that," I said. "You could have got that without even going to school. But do you think you could get a medal for something harder?"

"I bet I can," she said confidently. Sure enough, a little later she came home with a gold medal for French. "There you are," she said pertly. "I said I would, didn't I?"

Mrs. Kennedy and I both used to help her out when she got stuck with her homework, and it became a great joke with Caroline that I always got stuck with spelling, while her mother used to get tied up in knots over arithmetic.

"Oh, it's no use asking you to spell," Caroline would say. "I'd better ask Mummy."

When she took an arithmetic problem to her mother, Mrs. Kennedy would chew on her pencil for a bit, then pull a face of despair, whereupon Caroline would sigh and take the paper from her and trot over to me.

"Mummy's hopeless at mathematics, Miss Shaw. Can you help me, please?"

But it was never surprising to anyone who knew her that Caroline proved to be good at her schoolwork. She is naturally bright and attentive and studious. Even as a tot, she loved to curl up with a picture book. John, I know, is equally intelligent, but he is not as studious as his sister. He always much preferred horsing about to studying. While Caroline tends to be a little shy and reserved, John is outgoing and full of self-confidence.

He is the clown of the two, and a natural comic. I recall Mrs. Kennedy and me being in stitches one afternoon when John did his imitation of the Beatles. He stood there, swaying his hips, pretending to play the guitar and singing "She loves you, yeah-yeah-yeah" with a real sense of rhythm and tune. And John is as sharp as a tack, just like his sister. You could never put anything over on either of them. They both have their father's gift of asking just the right questions and pursuing their interrogation until they have the right answers to satisfy them. This is one of the reasons why I always answered their questions about their father truthfully and without trying to spin fairy tales. They wanted sensible answers from their mother and myself, and always got them.

Even at four and a bit, John was one hundred percent boy. He was much more interested in cowboys and Indians, guns, swords, soldiers, airplanes and space rockets than anything else. And he was just as bloodthirsty as any other boy. I remember his terrible impatience the time I took him to a children's theater. There was a character in the play who had an axe with which he kept threatening to chop people's heads off. Throughout the play, John kept nudging me.

"What does he keep holding the chopper for, Miss Shaw? Why doesn't he chop someone's head off?"

"Wait and see what happens," I whispered. A few minutes went by and then came another nudge.

"When is he going to use the chopper, Miss Shaw?"

"Shush," I said. "Wait and see." Actually, nobody got

his head chopped off, much to John's disgust, and he lamented the fact all the way home!

It was the same when we came to London and I took him to the ancient Tower of London, the traditional fortress of the city where the Queen keeps her Crown Jewels, and which is steeped in the history of England. John didn't want to see the Crown Jewels or the historic apartments. He spent his time looking at the cannons and swords, and when we got to the spot where executions used to be carried out, he was quite irrepressible. He wanted to know where the block was, where the executioner stood, how people rested their heads on the block and all the other gory details. As I say, it was all a bit bloodthirsty, but in my experience this is all part of a boy's growing up, and one has to put up with this passion for fighting and things like that which fascinate boys. It is much better to face the fact that they want to know about these things than to drag them away in the mistaken belief that it is unhealthy for a boy to ask about them. For it is not unhealthy—just natural.

In any case, on the other side of this lusty little fellow was a thoughtful, kind personality. You had to let him know who was boss, but you never had to urge him to be kind to his sister, for instance, since he shared his things with her and remembered her when he was given anything. And, if he did happen to hurt anyone's feelings and realized it, he was quick to make up for it.

New York proved to be a happy move for everyone. I could see, almost daily, how much Mrs. Kennedy improved in health and vitality. It was obvious from her face that she was gradually overcoming the horror of a year before. She smiled much more often now and, like the children, was able to talk about her husband quite normally. It was still work that was the best therapy for her. She had an office on Park Avenue from which she continued to answer the thousands of letters still coming in to her and to attend to the Kennedy Library, which is to be a living tribute to her husband.

There was also so much more for the children to do. Our apartment on Fifth Avenue was right across from Central Park, and there we spent many happy hours playing on the swings and seesaws and sailing boats on the lake. I knew a lot of other nurses in the city, and we used to meet regularly in the park in the mornings, each bringing our charges, of course, so John made many new friends. Caroline used to come with us in the afternoons when school was over. The Secret Service men carried the children's bicycles into the park for them, and together with Shannon—the dog—we all thoroughly enjoyed ourselves. Quite often, I took the children to the zoo cafeteria and bought them lunch out—a treat they really loved.

The Children's Zoo was another place they adored visiting. Their own two deer had been given to the zoo when they left the White House, and John could never get over the idea that they belonged to him and Caroline.

"They are *our* deer, aren't they, Miss Shaw?" he used to ask, half-expecting, I think, that I would tell him no.

Another expedition they loved to make was a trip to the Bronx Zoo, a much bigger place where they could go for camel rides and see the lions being fed—which John, of course, much preferred. Caroline was thrilled when she bought herself a key to the speaking boxes outside the animals' cages which switched on a tape recording, giving a short talk about the animal in question. When she bought the key, the man who handed it to her said: "There you are, the key to the zoo for life." Caroline was so excited about it, she couldn't wait to rush home and tell her mother she had the key to the zoo.

Caroline was delighted to find that she could still go riding in New York. Central Park has a riding strip and a stable where she could hire a horse for an hour or two —although keeping up with her on foot presented something of a problem to the Secret Service man.

Another advantage to New York was that many of the Kennedy children lived nearby. John and Caroline had their favorites, of course, among them. Caroline's great friend was Peter and Pat Lawford's daughter Sydney. She was about fifteen months older than Caroline, but they went to the same school in New York and saw each other every day. It was Sydney, more often than anyone, who came back to the apartment with us for dinner. Sydney was a great favorite with us all—a lovely golden-haired little girl with whom Caroline spent many, many happy hours.

The Lawfords lived only a couple of blocks from us in New York. The Smith family was also not far away from

185

us—Jean Kennedy Smith and her husband Stephen—
and it was from that family that John chose a firm friend.
This was little William Smith, who is now at the same
school as John.

In Hyannis Port, where the whole Kennedy clan gathered in summer, the children usually split up into two
age groups. With Caroline would be Sydney Lawford,
her brother Christopher, young Stephen Smith, who was
about seven months older than Caroline, and four of
Robert Kennedy's children—David, 11, Michael, 10,
Courtney, 8, and Mary-Kerry, 6. Then there were Eunice
and Sargent Shriver's children, Bobby and Maria. This
group was made up from the ones who were old enough
to go off riding and join in the more organized activities.

John's group consisted mainly of William Smith, the
Shrivers' boy Timmy and Teddy Kennedy's children,
Kara, 6, and Teddy, 4.

Caroline and Sydney were more like sisters than cousins. Sydney very often used to stay with us overnight in
the New York apartment. They were a great match in
personality and interests, frequently sitting opposite
each other at the table doing their homework, taking their
baths together, playing endless games with each other—
checkers, snakes and ladders and so on. It was always
very exciting for Caroline when Sydney was allowed to
stay overnight. Then, Caroline would personally supervise the preparation of the spare bed in her room for her
special schoolmate.

John, unfortunately, used to be a bit out of it until he, too, went to school. I recall him often trying to join in the games with his sister and Sydney, but as often as not he'd end up by tipping the checkers on the floor, much to Caroline's annoyance. However, when he started school and made friends with William, he had his own chum to play with. And you could always bet that it would be those two who would make all the noise. No snakes and ladders for them—more likely it would be cops and robbers!

The other favorites with the children were the Radziwills' children, Tony and Tina, whom they usually saw at Christmas. Caroline, particularly, really loved those two. Quite often, too, we invited children we met in the park home to the Fifth Avenue apartment for dinner. Mrs. Kennedy was very good about that. I always used to ask her beforehand, of course, but her reply was always the same.

"Certainly they can come," she would say. "I leave it to you. I like the children to have new friends. It's good for them."

She is very kind in that way, especially with anyone who takes an interest in her children. For example, earlier this year a pastrycook and his assistant came to the apartment, asking if they could have their photographs taken with the children. Now this would normally be an absurd request, and Mrs. Kennedy would not dream of doing it. But it happened that these men had for years sent the children a huge gingerbread house at Christmastime. It was always most beautifully decorated, and the children looked forward to its arrival every year and were never disappointed. However, when the man and his assistant asked permission to see the children, the Secret Service men, quite naturally, refused to let them up.

As a matter of routine, they called up to the fifteenth floor, where I happened to take the call in the apartment. Well, it was not for me to say what could happen, but I was always so impressed with the lovely gift which came every Christmas that I felt that perhaps Mrs. Kennedy would permit them up if she knew who they were. So I went in to see her. I told her who had called and what they wanted, and she gave her decision immediately.

"Oh, those kind and generous people," she said. "I have always wanted to know who sent that beautiful gingerbread house. Yes, send them up at once—I'm sure the children will be delighted."

We caught the men just as they were rather sadly leaving the front door and brought them back up to the apartment, where they took pictures with the children. Caroline and John were thrilled to bits at meeting the men who made their lovely gingerbread house.

The only things the children missed by being in New York were the long country rides we used to take out of Washington and—for John—visits to the airport to watch the planes taking off and landing. It took forever to get out into the country from the center of New York and John F. Kennedy Airport was pretty far away too. Still,

*188*

New York is a city where no one need ever be bored, and even on wet days we managed to make expeditions to museums and exhibitions, which the children enjoyed greatly, asking millions of questions that I struggled to answer as best I could.

But by far the best thing about New York was that Mrs. Kennedy and her children were left in peace. Here they were able to rehabilitate themselves and live almost normally, without being under the constant scrutiny of strangers and their ever-clicking cameras, or being pointed out to busloads of tourists, as happened in Washington. In New York, people seemed to accept the presence of the Kennedy children without staring at them or doing anything so ridiculous as asking for their autographs.

Naturally I was very glad to see the family regaining its equilibrium, to see Mrs. Kennedy looking more and more her old sparkling self, to see the children happily settled at their schools and a new pattern of life emerging for them all. But I was unhappy about something else. I knew that before long I would have to leave the children to return home to my family in Sheerness, where my sister and brother were both in ill health. I know that neither Jack nor Hettie will mind me saying that the decision to say good-bye to Mrs. Kennedy and her children—children I had come to love as much as I could love children of my own—was extremely difficult for me and caused me long restless nights.

Luckily, an invitation for Mrs. Kennedy and the children to come to England for the Kennedy Memorial Dedication at Runnymede provided an opportunity for me to say my good-byes on my own native soil. That, at least, made it a little easier for me.

# Chapter Seventeen

❀

❀    ❀

THROUGHOUT many sleepless nights and through many tears, I wrestled with the problem of when and how to leave Mrs. Kennedy and the children. At the beginning of 1965, I went home for a short holiday, and it was obvious that my own family needed me at home with them. This meant that at some time during the ensuing year, I would have to say good-bye to the family of which I had been a part for so long.

Yet the very idea of leaving Caroline and John made me so sad that I wept into my pillow, and spent hours standing at the window of the New York apartment, staring out at the millions of lights flashing and winking from the windows of the city. At such times, I found myself thinking back over seven years of warm, intimate memories of my life with the Kennedys. I told myself I had always known that it must end sometime, but now that the sometime was soon, I understood more than ever before that it was going to hurt me to say good-bye.

The beginning of the end came in New York when Mrs. Kennedy accepted the invitation for her and the children to visit England for the Runnymede ceremony. She thought at first that it would be easy for her to take care of the children by herself without my having to travel with them. Accordingly, she suggested that I might like to take the summer off and have a holiday in America—an idea that I accepted with great enthusiasm. Although I had been in America for some years, there were a great many places I had never seen, and I looked forward to roaming around the country for a month or so, rejoining the family when they returned from England and then talking with Mrs. Kennedy about my decision to leave.

But the whole plan was changed a couple of weeks later when Mrs. Kennedy and I were talking about her trip to England. She had just been having a long talk with the British Ambassador, Lord Harlech—a great friend of the Kennedys—and it appeared that nearly everyone in Britain wanted to meet her; her list of engagements was becoming longer and longer.

"I think I have underestimated this whole trip to England, Miss Shaw," she began. "It seems to me that there are so many things lined up for us that we are going to need you along with us. Would you mind?"

"Of course not," I said. "I'd be delighted." Then, at that moment, I realized that this trip would be an opportunity to say good-bye to Mrs. Kennedy and the children. I knew that sooner or later I would have to do it and go back home to Sheerness, and it might as well be sooner. I broached the subject to Mrs. Kennedy, and we talked it over together. We had a long discussion, and in a way, we both talked ourselves into agreement about it—she talked herself into realizing that she would not need me so much now that the children were both at school, and I talked myself out of a job.

"The children are going to be terribly upset," Mrs. Kennedy said. "How are you going to tell them?"

"I don't think I will tell them yet," I replied. "Let them think I am taking the summer off as planned, and then, when you leave Hyannis Port after the summer, I'll write and explain it to Caroline."

That was how we agreed to do it.

When I told Caroline that I was taking the summer off and would not be returning with her and John once they had been to England, she was quite put out. "Why can't you come back with us?" she wanted to know.

"Well, you know it is always a bit hectic at Hyannis Port, and I don't always enjoy that too much."

"But you like Newport," she replied. "Anyway, I hope this isn't going to happen every summer!" And she marched off almost huffily.

And so we left it at that. I did not really like not telling her the truth, but both Mrs. Kennedy and I thought that the children might be a bit upset and that it might spoil their trip to England.

*193*

Preparations for the visit were made amid great excitement. I had always told Caroline and John lots of things about my country and all there was to see in London, so together we made big plans to take in everything of interest. But the really important event of the visit was going to be meeting the Queen. This thrilled both the children to the utmost degree. Mrs. Kennedy decided it would be a good idea for them to practice how they should curtsy and bow to the Queen, and what they should say when presented.

"Miss Shaw will know what we have to do," Mrs. Kennedy told the children. "You just listen to her. She's English and she knows about those things."

So together we rehearsed the meeting with Queen Elizabeth. At first, I played the part of the Queen. Caroline curtsied to me and said: "Good afternoon, Your Majesty."

But poor John could never get the hang of it. He marched right up to me, made a beautiful bow and then said: "Good afternoon, My Majesty."

"No, John," I said. "That's not quite right. We have to call the Queen 'Your Majesty.' Try it again."

He looked a little puzzled, but he went back to the other end of the room, walked up to me again, bowed and repeated: "Good afternoon, My Majesty."

By this time, Caroline was in fits of giggles. Mrs. Kennedy was trying hard to hide her amusement as John defended himself indignantly. "You said she was *my* Majesty. That's what I said."

"Yes, I know that's what it sounds as if you ought to say," I explained, "but it is all a bit peculiar, and we have to say 'Your Majesty' when we meet the Queen." Finally, he got it right, but it never ceased to puzzle him.

Just before we left for England, I was asked to do something that I considered a great honor. It was to record my impressions of the late President as a father. This twenty-minute tape is to be put in the Kennedy Library at Cambridge, Massachusetts, along with other similar tributes, for the enjoyment and education of future generations. I was thrilled to be given this opportunity to tell people what a fine father John F. Kennedy was.

Flying over to England a week or two later was a nostalgic time for us all, for we traveled in the Presidential jet—the same aircraft on which we had flown so many times before. It brought back memories of holiday trips to Palm Beach and Hyannis with the President and his family during those wonderful White House days. For the children, it meant heaps of chewing gum and candy again and—for John especially—the sheer delight at being back on "Daddy's airplane." The same Air Force sergeant who had always looked after us was still in the crew, and the children recognized him as an old friend. We flew over with the President's brothers Robert and Edward, Secretary of State Dean Rusk and a whole retinue of important people, but the atmosphere on board the plane was that of a holiday trip, and we all thoroughly enjoyed ourselves.

Even Mrs. Kennedy caught the spirit of lightheartedness, and during the flight she remarked quite happily: "This brings back some wonderful memories, doesn't it?" And then, quietly: "There is only one person missing. . . ."

Once we landed in England, we were met by crowds of dignitaries, and poor Mrs. Kennedy must have been quite worn out by the time we drove in convoy to London and the home of Prince Radziwill in Buckingham Place, where she and the children were staying. Caroline and John were terribly excited at being in England and seeing some of the things I had described to them. On the way to London they saw their first English policeman, got used to being driven on the "wrong" side of the road, caught a glimpse of Buckingham Palace and the red-coated guards in the forecourt—they could hardly wait to begin the exciting round of sightseeing they had been promised for so long.

It was a great pity that Mrs. Kennedy was not always able to come with the children when we "did" the town, but she was quite firm with me about taking the children out.

"You must take them and show them all the things you used to tell us about, Miss Shaw," she said. "I'll catch up with you when I can."

So, the day after we arrived, we began a wonderful series of outings. We fed the ducks in Green Park, saw the Changing of the Guard, went to the zoo in Regent's Park, walked down Piccadilly, and toured the Tower of London. Caroline also went riding in Rotten Row. She did this several times, and during our visits to the riding stables in Hyde Park, she showed just what she could get away with by being her charming little self. After two or three rides on borrowed horses, Caroline looked wistfully at the horse owned by the woman in charge of the stables.

"I sure wish I could ride your horse," she said.

"Oh dear," said the woman, "I'm afraid I never let anyone else ride him."

Caroline just smiled and said no more. But a couple of days later, there she was, riding the animal. She had won the day with her own brand of charm, plus her obvious expertise in the saddle.

But before we really got under way with our Grand Tour, there was the most important item on the agenda— the ceremony at Runnymede, where Her Majesty the Queen dedicated a memorial stone and a small plot of English soil to the memory of President Kennedy.

For me, this was a wonderful moment. I had not even expected to attend the ceremony, but Mrs. Kennedy decided that it would be a good idea for me to be close at hand to keep an eye on the children—or rather, on John. For if anyone was going to act up or get restless during the proceedings, it was going to be this little scamp. So, I found myself appointed to a seat in the grandstand adjacent to the row in which Mrs. Kennedy and Queen Elizabeth were seated. It turned out to be a privilege that I did not really deserve, for John was as good as gold throughout, and I was hardly needed.

There was only one moment during that afternoon when the smoothly formulated arrangements left me a bit high and dry, and that was when everyone returned to Windsor Castle for tea. I found myself standing in the courtyard, not quite knowing whether I ought to go up with the children, or wait until they had taken tea and rejoin them later. I decided to take the second course, since I did not want to embarrass anyone by appearing to gate-crash the tea party. I was chatting to one of the foot-men in the courtyard when a young girl came out looking for me. She turned out to be Prince Andrew's nurse, and she was kindness itself to me.

"Come up and have a cup of tea with me," she said. "We'll have it upstairs on our own—unless you'd rather take tea with the official party. You can if you like."

"No, I'd rather not," I said.

"Good," she replied. "I'm glad, because if you went, I'd have to go, and it's all a bit starchy."

I followed her up the stairs, but to my utter surprise, we met the Queen coming down.

"Excuse me, Your Majesty," said the young nurse. "I am just taking Miss Shaw upstairs for a cup of tea."

"Certainly, that's all right," the Queen replied.

After tea, and a chat about our respective charges, I came downstairs again to meet up with Mrs. Kennedy, Caroline and John. They were in the hallway when I came down, and Mrs. Kennedy was talking to the Queen as Caroline came over to me. The next moment Mrs. Kennedy motioned me quietly to join her. I walked across, thinking she wanted to give me some instruction or other about taking charge of the children. I was completely taken aback when she spoke.

"Your Majesty," she said to the Queen, "I would like to introduce Miss Shaw, who looks after my children."

I was so overwhelmed, I cannot for the life of me remember anything the Queen said to me or what I talked about, but I felt tremendously touched at Mrs. Kennedy's charming and thoughtful gesture.

I was also introduced to Prince Philip, and as we shook hands, I wondered if he remembered how we had met briefly, eighteen months before, in much more harrowing circumstances. This was at the time of the President's funeral when he, along with other heads of state, had come back to the White House for some refreshment. For some reason, I had to chase after John along the second-floor corridor, and I was hurrying after him when I saw a half-familiar figure come out of the sitting-room door.

For a moment, I was unable to place the face—and anyway, I was more concerned with taking John in hand. The kind-looking man watched me catch up with John, turn, and lead him back to the nursery. As I passed him again, he spoke.

"I've got one like that," he grinned. "They're a handful, aren't they?"

"Heavens, you're right," I said casually, and walked on.

It was only after another dozen steps that I suddenly

remembered that lean, suntanned face. It was Prince Philip! Horrified at the way I had spoken so casually, I turned round to make some apology—but he had gone. No doubt the incident had long since faded from his memory, but it was on my mind all the time I was at Windsor that memorable afternoon in May.

But if that afternoon was the big moment of the fortnight for me, John's came when we went to see the Changing of the Guard and to visit the Tower of London. At the Horse Guard's Parade, he was quite entranced by the sight of the magnificent cavalrymen with their shining breastplates, swords and plumed helmets. For a while, at any rate, the Life Guards replaced the U.S. Marines and the astronauts as favorites in this little fellow's mind. When the ceremony was over, Caroline was in raptures about the horses the soldiers had ridden.

"Weren't they wonderful horses, Miss Shaw?" she said.

"Huh!" John snorted. "I liked the *soldiers*."

At the Tower, where we met the Governor and had tea with his children, John was equally scathing about the Crown Jewels and the ancient apartments. As I mentioned before, his big interest was the execution site.

He pestered the life out of the kindly old Beefeater sergeant who showed us around, asking all the bloodthirsty questions about the executions. Then he had a field day among the cannons, guns, suits of armor and swords in the exhibition galleries. Caroline was a little appalled at her brother, but, as usual, she joined in his

*200*

fun and dutifully crawled through the barrel of one of the cannons when John urged her.

"Come on, Caroline," he piped. "Let's crawl through here."

"It's a bit dirty," Caroline said doubtfully.

"Oh, come *on*," he said, and the next thing we knew, we could only see his feet sticking out of one end. We hurried round to the front of the gun to see his face—absolutely radiant with delight—pop out of the other end.

At the London Zoo, they put on a special chimps' tea party for us, and the performance of these friendly little animals playing about with teapots, cups and saucers made Caroline screech with laughter.

"Oh, Miss Shaw, what table manners!" she said, when one chimp poured his tea over his neighbor. She clapped her hand over her mouth in a typical Caroline gesture, her big eyes popping with the excitement of it all.

When we had been in London for about a week, Mrs. Kennedy asked me if I were going home to Sheerness during the trip. I said I would like to do that.

"Well, why don't you take the children with you?" she said. "I know they would love to see your brother and sister, after all you have said about them."

"Oh, I'd love to take them," I said. "May they stay the weekend and sleep at the house?"

"Certainly," Mrs. Kennedy said. "They'd like that."

So we packed our weekend cases and went down to Sheerness in a big embassy car, complete with two Special Branch men from Scotland Yard and one of our own

Secret Service agents. And that was quite a trip for us all. To begin with, we were chased all over the place by pressmen, which meant whizzing up and down the streets of Sheerness pursued by carloads of photographers. John thought this was tremendous fun and kept urging the driver to go faster and faster—a cry which, I am glad to say, went unheeded! Caroline, too, took it all as a great game. Once, when we had to run the gauntlet of the photographers, she pulled all her hair down over her face as she ran. When she got indoors, she grinned and said: "I fooled them, Miss Shaw. They'll only have a picture of my hair, won't they, Stan?" Stan was one of the Special Branch men to whom Caroline took a big liking. Every time we went out, she wanted to know if Stan was coming with us, and she was only too happy to trot along holding his hand. Both these children always won the affection of the people with them.

John was quite satisfied with our little terraced house. When we got to James Street, Sheerness, and went into the house to meet Hettie and Jack, he took one quick look around and pronounced: "I like this dumpy little house, Miss Shaw. I'm glad you have only one flight of stairs. I'm tired of stairs." (At the Radziwills', he had to go up four flights to his bedroom.)

"You're Hettie and you're Jack," he said when he met my sister and brother. "How do you do? I'm John F. Kennedy, Junior." He nosed about for a little while, and then asked Hettie:

"Where's the cook and the butler?"

"I'm the cook and butler around here," replied Hettie.

"You can't be the butler, too," he said. "You're not a man."

"Well, I do all the work," replied Hettie.

"Good. That means Miss Shaw won't have to do any work," he said, highly satisfied at the state of affairs in the household.

Of course, he made himself completely at home from the moment he walked in. Caroline was a little more shy, but she got on famously with Hettie and Jack, proudly telling them that she was my blood sister for life.

We had a very happy couple of days in my little home. We played games, went down to the beach to look for cockles, chased through the crowds of sightseers, slept in makeshift beds and laughed a lot. But throughout, I was painfully aware of the awful fact that my days with these two lovely children were running out fast. They knew nothing about that, of course, thinking only that I was staying on in England for a holiday. I couldn't tell them, even then. These two, the children of one of the greatest men in the world, went to sleep that night in their beds in the tiny house I called home, and as I watched them, I could do nothing but weep.

I said my farewells to them a couple of days later in Prince Radziwill's house, shortly before they were due to drive to the airport and return to America. Caroline, I am sure, suspected something was amiss, for she followed me around the whole morning with her arm around me, quieter than usual.

John wanted to know: "Won't you just come back as far as New York with us?"

"I'll come back a little later," I said. "I'm going back to see Hettie and Jack for a while."

I said good-bye to Caroline and John in the living room. John looked at me with big eyes when I gave him his good-bye kiss, still asking if I couldn't go back with him. Caroline hugged me tightly, and I held her in my arms, telling her to be a good girl and look after John for me.

"Will I still be your bestest friend when you get back?" she asked.

"Of course you will. You'll always be my bestest friend. We're blood sisters, aren't we?" I said.

When I came to say good-bye to Mrs. Kennedy, we were both more than a little upset. After seven years, it was not easy for either of us to part for good—as only we knew it would be.

"Caroline is so upset about your not coming back," Mrs. Kennedy said. "Can't you come with us, even now?" Terribly torn, even at the eleventh hour, between my own family and the children I loved, I could only shake my head sadly.

"You will promise to come back and visit us every year?" Mrs. Kennedy asked.

"Yes, I will," I said.

"Then this is not good-bye—you are not to go out of our lives . . . au revoir."

I don't remember saying anything else. I don't think I

was capable of speaking, feeling as utterly miserable as I did. I couldn't bear to see the children again, and was well out of the way when they went to the airport. It was so sad. The thought of "my bestest friend" and "my big boy" making their lives in the future without me hurt badly—affected me more deeply than I can ever describe.

I went back home then. It took me a week to unpack my things, because every time I walked up the stairs to my room and stood alone, surrounded by the photographs I treasure of the Kennedy family, I simply burst into tears.

I have tried in these pages to recount some of the happiness and rewards I have known in the years I have spent looking after other people's children, particularly Caroline and John Kennedy. But no words can ever really tell how closely bound I felt toward these two and their parents.

For seven years, I was part of them. And they will always be part of me.

## ABOUT THE AUTHOR

As a young girl, Maud Shaw took her first job as governess in order to earn her own money and be independent of her family. Through her career, she has traveled all over the world—from Malta, where she was raised, to Germany, England, Cyprus, South Africa, and the United States. When, in 1957, Mrs. Jacqueline Kennedy, wife of the Democratic Senator from Massachusetts, asked Miss Shaw to take care of her first child which was expected in December, she accepted. This was the beginning of seven and a half extraordinary years with the Kennedys. Miss Shaw retired in 1965, and now lives with her brother and sister in Sheerness, Kent, England.